HONG KONG

William Collins Sons & Co. Ltd
London • Glasgow • Sydney • Auckland
Toronto • Johannesburg

British Library Cataloguing in Publication Data

Collins Illustrated Guide to Hong Kong — (China Guides Series)
1. Hong Kong — Description and travel
— Guidebooks
I. Series
915.1′25045   DS796.H74

ISBN 0-00-215226-6

First published under the title *A Guide to Hong Kong* 1987
Revised and reprinted 1988
Copyright © The Guidebook Company Ltd 1981, 1986, 1989

Text by Caroline Courtauld and Jill Hunt
Revised by Jane Ram, Stephanie and Chris Holmes
Additional text contributions by Jane Ram, Chris and Stephanie Holmes, Clive Viney, David Bonavia, D.A. Griffiths, Harry Rolnick and Shann Davies
Series Editors: May Holdsworth and Sallie Coolidge
Picture Editor: Carolyn Watts

Printed in Hong Kong

Photography by Airphoto International (22, 92−93, 148−149, 168−169, 206−207); China Guides Series (11, 15, 18−19, 35, 38, 39, 42−43, 46, 47, 50, 54−55, 70, 75, 78, 88, 98, 129, 140, 153, 156, 177); Alain Evrard, Stock House (62); Greg Girard (67 lower right, 102−103, 110−111, 126−127, 136−137, 144−145, 160−161, 164−165, 173, 180, 188, 194−195); Joan Law (81); James Montgomery (58−59, 66−67 left and upper right, 123, 199); Jacky Yip, China Photo Library (202−203); Carolyn Watts (30−31); Wong Chun Wai (6−7).

Cover photograph by Airphoto International

Collins Illustrated Guide to

HONG KONG

by
Caroline Courtauld and Jill Hunt

Revised by
Jane Ram, Stephanie and Chris Holmes

COLLINS

8 Grafton Street, London W1
1988

HONG KONG

(Preceding pages)Hong Kong Island and Kowloon by night

Contents

Special Topics

Maps

Names and Addresses

The spelling of Chinese names in this guide follows the Wade-Giles system prevalent in Hong Kong and not the *Pinyin* system now used in Mainland China.

All prices are quoted in Hong Kong dollars.

An Introduction

Hong Kong is something of a kaleidoscope. Look! Enjoy! Turn, and
you see something totally different, but equally captivating.

Arrival in Hong Kong must stir even the most blasé traveller. The
approach to Kai Tak Airport is always dramatic. According to the
prevailing weather, you may skim over the rooftops of Kowloon to
reach the runway with a faint whiff of soy sauce and garlic still clinging
to the undercarriage. Or you may soar arrogantly over the steep-sided
mountains, harshly indented coastline and thriving harbour to find the
runway projecting out into the sea like a great grey and green welcome
carpet. At night the most densely-packed parts of Hong Kong take on
their own magic, as millions of lights transform even the most squalid
buildings into part of a gigantic fairyland.

First acquaintance can be exhilarating, or disastrous — there are
few half-tones in Hong Kong. The general pace is frenetic, everyone
pushing along to get somewhere ahead of the crowd: unfortunately
another 5.5 million people work on the same principle, and the result
is endless jostling. Only the newcomer or the visitor stands at street
corners, uncertain which way to turn, or has leisure to look around and
actually see the dramatic combination of mountains and water, echoed
in the patterns of high-rise buildings and roads everywhere. If you
don't like what you see, change your vantage point and sooner or later
you will find something in Hong Kong to which you can relate. And in
a place which measures only 1,070 square kilometres, the looking is
part of the fun.

Hong Kong has no equivalent to the Parthenon or the Great Wall
— although the ever denser lines of skyscrapers come close to
Wonders-of-the-World status. The place offers no more — and no less
— than itself, a total experience, unlike any other.

Its duty free status has long made shopping one of Hong Kong's
premier attractions. Vast areas seem to be nothing but shops large and
small, stretching for miles to form the world's most extensive bazaar.
In case you wondered, bargains still exist: rare antiques, breathtaking
silks, jewellery fit for a queen, the latest high-tech stereo, computer
and photographic wizardry, simple regional handicrafts with a rustic
charm all their own. Hong Kong's shops have these and more.

If you spend much time shopping, you can't help noticing
something of another favourite Hong Kong activity — eating. The
variety of foods from different regions of China is staggering. But
Hong Kong's culinary delights extend to impeccably prepared and
served French haute cuisine; pizza and pasta redolent of the
Mediterranean; fiery Indian, Thai or Indonesian specialities and a

thousand and one other delights from around the world. Yes, you will even find franchise hamburgers and fish-and-chips (albeit wrapped in Chinese-language newspapers).

Hong Kong has many faces. It can be uncompromisingly Westernised, totally urban, with little to distinguish it from big cities anywhere in the world. But step away from the main road with its glittering showcases and mirror-fronted commercial buildings. Find a more personal side of life: a shrine blackened by countless clouds of burning incense as it wafts messages to the next world; a building from the early years of this century given a new lease of life and standing happily alongside its mighty neighbours; an alley of songbirds in dainty bamboo cages, or bubbling aquaria filled with magnificent ornamental fish patiently awaiting the connoisseurs who gather every day to admire the latest stock; an invisible mender, one of the last of these dedicated souls who can repair a tear or a moth-hole to make a much-treasured garment as good as new; a craftsman carving soapstone seals in the same spot where his father, and his grandfather, worked before him; countrywomen chanting a unique counting song as they unload fresh eggs for a wholesaler; a fruit stall, laden with the best and freshest from the orchards of the world, where the owner will squeeze a glassful of fresh orange juice or peel a crisp Tianjin pear for you on the spot.

While Hong Kong has some of the world's most intensely populated areas, where housing barely justifies that name, it also has wide open spaces, where you can walk for a day and scarcely see another human being. Three-quarters of the land is undeveloped and almost half is designated officially as country parks. Awesome mountain ranges, ancient *fung shui* woods, rare wild orchids, pre-historic rock carvings, an egretry and a unique wet-land nature reserve are only some of the less well-known features of Hong Kong which can be found with a modicum of initiative.

Arriving in Hong Kong

The Airport Like many of Hong Kong's public facilities, Kai Tak
Airport barely has been able to keep up with the expanding numbers
of users. Massive expansion is under way, and there is even talk of a
second airport, with other international airports in China just to the
north of the border and also in Macau. But for the moment, arriving
passengers should expect a minimum of half an hour to come through
Customs and Immigration, and at peak times formalities may take an
hour or more.

The terminal building, with its busy concourses and minimum of
seating, is designed for efficient passenger handling. In the pre-
departure areas you must keep an eye on the computerized departure
boards because there are no public announcements of flight
departures. An airport tax of HK$100 ($50 for children under 12 years
old) is charged when leaving Hong Kong.

For the benefit of arriving passengers, helpful information counters
are run by the Hong Kong Tourist Association (HKTA), the Hong
Kong Hotels Association (which will book rooms for you), and the
Hong Kong Association of Travel Agents. No matter what your
budget, it is always sensible to reserve accommodation in advance:
Hong Kong's increasing importance as a base for doing business with
China means many hotels are full virtually all year round.

Transport to and from the Airport

Taxis (make sure the driver uses the meter) can be hired just beyond
the arrivals hall at two well-disciplined queues. Regular **airport bus**
services run from the airport to Tsimshatsui, in Kowloon, and to
Central and Causeway Bay on Hong Kong Island. Number A1 goes
along Nathan Road past or close to most Tsimshatsui hotels for a flat
charge of HK$5 (8 am – 10.30 pm); and number A2 (HK$7) goes as far
as the Victoria Hotel to the west of Central, while the A3 (HK$7)
circles most Causeway Bay hotels. Put the correct amount in the
driver's box as you enter — no change is given on the bus, but you can
obtain change from the nearby kiosk or in the airport. Many hotels
have their own airport buses. Contact a hotel representative outside
the customs hall, or ask at the Hong Kong Hotels Association desk.

Although Kai Tak is very near the city centre, roads can be
congested and you should allow at least half an hour to get to the
airport from Tsimshatsui and an hour from Central during morning
and evening rush hours. At other times it takes less than 20 minutes
from either area.

General Information for Travellers

Visas Visa requirements differ, depending upon nationality. Visitors from most countries can enter Hong Kong without a visa for periods varying from seven days to six months. U.S. citizens can stay for a month without a visa, while Commonwealth citizens can stay up to three months. Visitors from western European countries fall either into the three-month or one-month category. U.K. citizens with passports issued in Britain do not need visas at all — when they first arrive a stay of six months is normally granted, and an extension is usually easily obtained.

All visitors must hold valid travel documents, and should be able to show they have enough funds to cover their stay in Hong Kong, and an onward, or return, ticket. Residents must register for an Identity Card and must carry the card or some other proof of identity at all times. Visitors are technically exempt from this regulation, but in your own interests you would be well advised to carry your passport or other similar document wherever you go in Hong Kong.

Customs As a free trade centre, Hong Kong allows most items to be carried in duty free. The only dutiable items are tobacco, alcohol, cosmetics and petroleum products. Duty-free allowances for visitors are: 200 cigarettes, 50 cigars, or 250 grams (half pound) of tobacco; one quart of alcohol; perfume in reasonable quantities. Firearms (that is, personal property such as rifles and revolvers) must be declared and handed into custody until departure.

Vaccinations No vaccinations are required unless you have been in a cholera or smallpox infected area within the preceding 14 days.

Climate and Clothing

Hong Kong has a climate with distinct seasons. A long, hot and humid summer with heavy rain contrasts with a drier and cooler (occasionally chilly) winter. Autumn varies from a few weeks to three or four months, and spring may be no more than a few days. By far the most pleasant weather is during autumn and early winter, from October to the end of December. Skies are clear and blue, the humidity lower (around 70 percent), and there is little rain. Temperatures during the day reach the mid-20s °C (high 60s °F) and rarely fall below 10°C (50°F) in the evening.

January and February are the coldest months — temperatures as low as 0°C (32°F) have been recorded in the northern New Territories, although the mean average is around 16°C (61°F). In February, the humidity begins to rise again; March and April are often damp and depressing, with low clouds and mist obscuring even the lower hills, there is little sunshine and increasingly higher temperatures. This is the season when residents complain of mildewed leather, soggy newspapers and walls running with condensation.

By May, summer has begun. For the next four or five months temperatures usually reach 30°C−32°C (86°F−90°F) every day, without dropping noticeably at night. Three-quarters of the annual rainfall occurs in this period, often in heavy outbursts, but there is plenty of hot sun too — an average of 240 hours in June. Humidity is 90 percent or more. By August, the season for typhoons (tropical storms with winds of hurricane force) begins. There are few direct hits, but even from 100 miles away, a typhoon can do considerable damage. The Royal Observatory, with its new satellite ground station, can provide extremely accurate information on the whereabouts of the cyclone centre and the maximum wind speeds. The public receives plenty of warning via the Observatory's series of signals. These are hoisted at various points throughout the Colony and announced at frequent intervals on television and radio. Number 1 warns that a tropical storm is within 400 nautical miles of Hong Kong and may affect the territory. Number 3 means the storm is approaching Hong Kong and winds of at least 22 knots, which may gust to 60 knots, may be expected within 12 hours. At this point shops and hotels start erecting storm shutters, boats go into typhoon shelters and ferries to outlying islands may be cancelled at short notice. At Number 8 (rarely hoisted more than once or twice a year) schools are closed and all offices must close to allow workers to return home before public transport stops. Shops shut and just about everything comes to a standstill. Number 10 (a rare occurrence) indicates that a typhoon has hit town with hurricane winds of 64 knots or more.

What to Wear Visitors usually find the Hong Kong Chinese well dressed and fashion conscious. Air-conditioning is virtually universal in hotels, restaurants and the larger shops; nonetheless, lightweight clothes are essential for summer. An umbrella is useful for wet weather; a raincoat is often unbearably sticky in the high humidity. Men can wear light trousers and shirts on most occasions during summer, although jackets and ties are advisable for some business appointments and are mandatory in a few smart restaurants. They are also required in some hotel bars such as the Mandarin's Captain's Bar in the evening. Central heating is rare in winter. Bring some warm clothes — sweaters, jackets and a light overcoat, gloves and possibly a hat or scarf — if you are visiting Hong Kong in December through March.

Money

Currency As the financial centre of Asia, Hong Kong has over 156 licensed banks from 11 countries. Bank of America, Citibank, Chase Manhattan, Banque Nationale de Paris, Barclays International, Bank of Tokyo — to name a few — all have several branches. A comprehensive network of local banks as well as the Bank of China covers the territory. Banking hours are from 9.30 or 10 am to 3 pm, with some banks staying open as late as 6 pm.

There is no central bank in Hong Kong. The local Hongkong and Shanghai Banking Corporation — established in 1864 by Hong Kong-based merchants — and the London-based Standard Chartered Bank issue the territory's banknotes in denominations of $1,000, $500, $100, $50, $20 and $10; in addition there are $5, $2, $1, 50 cents, 20 cents and 10 cents coins. Large old-style banknotes are being replaced by smaller ones and currently two sizes are in circulation. Hong Kong currency can be freely imported or exported.

Exchange Currencies and travellers cheques can be changed at any bank or at hotels (where the rate tends to be less favourable) and at the many money changers in the business district, such as Lark International Finance Limited, which has branches in Swire House and Shell House. Most shops frequented by tourists will also accept payment in hard foreign currencies. Since October 1983 the Hong Kong dollar has been pegged to the US dollar at an exchange rate of HK$7.78/7.79:US$1. Some sample exchange rates for major currencies at the end of February, 1988 were:

£1	HK$13.75	1SW Krona	HK$1.23
Can$1	HK$6.15	1DM	HK$4.59
A$1	HK$5.60	1FF	HK$1.35
		1 Dutch Guilder	HK$4.09

Credit cards Credit cards are widely accepted, although shops are more likely to offer a discount for payment by cash or personal local cheque.

Tipping Restaurants, bars and hotels generally add a 10 percent service charge to bills, but it is customary to leave small change for the waiters. For short trips within the city taxi drivers do not expect a tip, elsewhere five to 10 percent is normal. The going rate for porters at the airport is HK$5 per piece of luggage. Hotel bell-boys expect HK$5 per bag carried. At barber shops and hairdressers a reasonable tip is 10 percent of the bill.

Language

For all its veneer of Western sophistication, Hong Kong is unequivocally Chinese where language is concerned. The main Chinese dialect is Cantonese, which is as different from Mandarin, generally spoken throughout mainland China, as French is from Italian. Minority dialects include Shanghainese, Chiu Chow and Hakka.

Officially, English has equal status with Chinese, as reflected in bilingual road signs, public notices, and business and government documents. However, comprehension of English is limited among people you will encounter on public transport, and in shops and restaurants outside international hotels or those accustomed to catering to the local expatriate community. Taxi drivers can be relied on to recognise English names for obvious tourist destinations, but if directed anywhere off the beaten track they may take you to the nearest police station for help, or simply ask you to try another taxi. They can sometimes be persuaded to use their radio-phone to call for directions. The situation is complicated by the haphazard translations of street names. Some are literal translations of the English words, whereas others are approximate phonetic equivalents of what the English words sound like in Chinese. For example, 'Fa Yuen Do' literally means 'Garden Road', whereas 'Wan Hum Gai' is a transliteration based on the mispronunciation of 'Wyndham Street'. The adventurous tourist would be well advised to get a hotel receptionist to write out his intended destination in Chinese characters, or to carry a street index which gives English and Chinese place names.

The Hong Kong Tourist Association

Tourism is big business in Hong Kong. More than 4.5 million visitors poured into the colony in 1987, spending some HK$25.4 billion on goods and services — a 42 percent increase over the previous year. Responsibility for the smooth running of this important industry rests with the Hong Kong Tourist Association (HKTA), a statutory body 90 percent subsidised by government, which co-ordinates the activities of the city and advises on development.

Efficient and helpful service have won the HKTA a favourable reputation among visitors. If you need advice or information, it is always worth trying the HKTA first. Facilities include a telephone information service (tel. 5-244191 Monday—Friday and public holidays 8 am—6 pm; Saturday and Sunday 8 am—1 pm) and four information centres: Star Ferry Concourse in Kowloon, by the ferry entrance

(Monday—Friday and public holidays 8 am—6 pm; Saturday and
Sunday 8 am—1 pm); Government Publications Centre, General Post
Office Building, Central, Hong Kong (just to the west of the Star
Ferry entrance, Monday—Friday 9 am—6 pm; Saturday 9 am—1 pm);
35th Floor, Connaught Centre, Central, Hong Kong (just to the west
of the Star Ferry entrance, opposite the General Post Office,
Monday—Friday 8 am—6 pm; Saturday 8 am—1 pm); Kai Tak Airport,
Buffer Hall for arriving passengers (daily 10 am—10 pm).

There are also representative offices in the U.S., Europe and
Australia. Cathay Pacific Airways represent the Association in other
areas.

The HKTA publishes a great deal of literature, including a useful
tourist map and a series of leaflets, frequently updated, on shopping,
hotels, beaches, museums, walks and other tourist topics. Their free
pocket *Official Guidebook* is disappointingly padded out with
advertisements, but the *Official Guide to the Best of Hong Kong
Shopping* contains an indispensable list of all the HKTA-approved
shops (some 1,300 of them) and restaurants, together with a selected
directory of services visitors may need, and some useful maps. They
also publish a weekly newspaper, *The Orient*, mostly useful for its
practical information and 'What's On' column.

The familiar HKTA sign — a red junk enclosed in a white circle —
indicates that the member is nominally bound to 'maintain ethical
standards' and to 'discourage malpractices contrary to the best
interests of visitors'. The HKTA investigates any complaints against
their members (which should be made by telephoning 5-244191 ext.
278) and can terminate anyone's membership if appropriate. They will
also initiate legal action against a member who has cheated visitors.

Telephone

Hong Kong's subscribers do not pay for local calls, so phones are free
in most hotel lobbies, restaurants and shops. A visitor need only ask to
use one. Public call boxes exist in many places and it costs HK$1 to
phone anywhere in the territory. If you dial from Kowloon to Hong
Kong Island you must use the prefix 5. For the New Territories the
prefix is 0. To dial to Kowloon from Hong Kong or the New
Territories you must use the prefix 3. If you are dialling within the
same area, omit the prefix, for instance when dialling Kowloon
numbers from Kowloon.

Getting around Hong Kong

The transport system of the world's most densely populated metropolis is, predictably, highly complex, and in a state of perpetual modernisation and expansion. A fast-growing population, the engineering problems caused by steep mountain slopes, a bedrock of decomposed granite and the 0.75-mile stretch of water between the two main urban centres all conspire to create a transport planner's nightmare.

For the visitor, these problems have resulted in a delightfully wide range of transport which is well worth trying. However, in a territory where there are too many cars for the meagre 693 miles of road, traffic congestion is a perennial problem. Just about all forms of public transport are packed during rush hours (7.30−9.30 am and 5−6.30 pm). And on fine Sundays or public holidays ferries to outlying islands and all means of getting to the New Territories and to the beaches are equally crowded. If you want to be comfortable, you must simply avoid travelling at these times.

Taxis

Hong Kong taxis are cheap by international standards, and in most places they can be easily hailed in the street except at particular times of day (around 4 pm when drivers change over, and during rush hours). If you are caught in Central at these times, make for a taxi rank, such as the one at Star Ferry or by the Mass Transit Railway's Admiralty Station.

Taxi drivers are all licensed and the cars are metered. Flagfall is HK$5.50 for the first two kilometres, with an additional charge of HK70 cents for every 0.25 kilometre thereafter. An additional HK$20 is charged if the cross-harbour tunnel is used, HK$3.50 for the Aberdeen tunnel. A second taxi service (using green and white cars, instead of the urban red and silver ones) is restricted to the rural areas in the New Territories. Flagfall for these taxis is HK$4.50 for the first two kilometres and 90 cents per 0.4 kilometre thereafter. A very small fleet of taxis and hire cars operates on Lantau Island, based around Silvermine Bay.

Most drivers understand enough English to get you to the better-known destinations, although Kowloon drivers tend to be vague about Hong Kong Island, and vice versa. And if you do have a problem with an unco-operative driver, note the time and number of the taxi and contact the HKTA or the police, who will pass on your complaint to a special centre.

Ferries

Ferries are a major form of transport in Hong Kong. Services go from Hong Kong to all the major outlying islands; others link different points on both sides of Victoria Harbour (see the map on page 26). Hover ferry services run to Cheung Chau and to Tsuen Wan, as well as to Macau.

The most famous service is offered by the Star Ferry Company, whose chunky green-and-white boats have been plying between Central and Tsimshatsui since the end of the last century. For atmosphere — and value for money — this seven-minute journey would be hard to beat anywhere in the world. Passengers pay at a turnstile — HK80 cents for first class (top deck), HK60 cents for second class (lower deck). The Star Ferry operates between 6.30 am and 11.30 pm. Passengers never have to wait more than a few minutes, except in the early morning and late at night on Sundays when departures are at 20-minute intervals. The company also plies a route between Central and Hunghom — a very convenient way to reach the Coliseum and Hunghom Railway Terminus.

Over and above the regular cross-harbour services, the Star Ferry runs six one-hour cruises daily: Noon Day Gun starts at 11.15 am; Seafarers at 12.30 pm; Seabreezes at 2.15 pm; Afternoon Tea at 3.30 pm; Sundowner at 7 pm; and Harbour Lights at 9.15 pm. The ticket price of HK$50 ($40 for children) covers souvenirs and unlimited free drinks. Departure is from the Star Ferry Kowloon pier and 10 minutes later from the Hong Kong pier. You can buy tickets at the piers or through travel agents, or telephone 3-669878/3-7318483 for further information.

Ferries to the largest of Hong Kong's outlying islands, run by the Hong Kong and Yaumati Ferry Company, leave from the bustling, shabby Outlying Districts Ferry Pier in Central. Tickets are on sale about half an hour before departure — there are different ticket offices for each route. Queues form early at weekends (when many fares double, so it is best to travel mid-week). Once on the boat to Lantau or Cheung Chau, it is very pleasant to sit out on the deluxe class open sun deck. Both Hong Kong Island and the mainland look magnificent from the sea, at night as well as in the daytime. And there is a wealth of other craft to look at — huge passenger liners, cargo vessels, jetfoils to Macau, fishing junks at work, and, if you are lucky, a deep sea fishing junk with bat-wing sails spread wide.

Fares are HK$6.50 for deluxe class on a weekday trip to Lantau (one hour and 15 minutes) and only HK$4.50 for the lower second class deck, which has no air-conditioning or open sun deck. There are

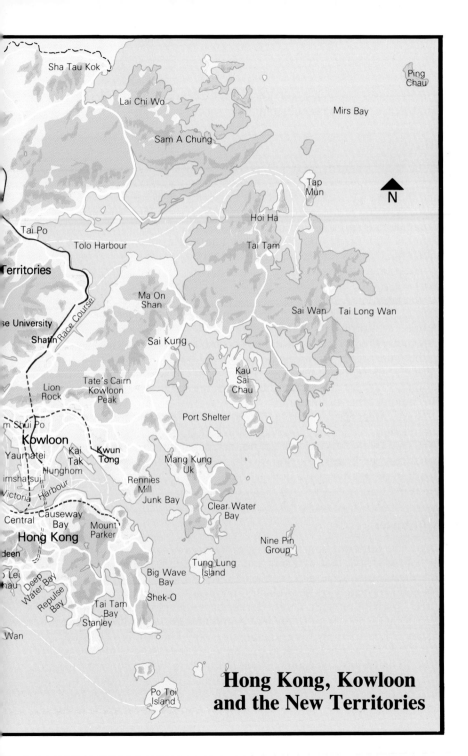

Hong Kong, Kowloon and the New Territories

toilet facilities on board, and tea, coffee, beer, soft drinks, dry sandwiches, instant noodles and other snacks are sold.

Buses

Hong Kong's heavily used bus network reaches most corners of the Territory. Buses are run by three private companies — in Kowloon and the New Territories, the Kowloon Motor Bus Company operates more than 200 routes; on Hong Kong Island, the China Motor Bus Company has some 100 routes, with additional cross-harbour buses run together with the KMB; and the New Lantau Bus Company runs a much smaller bus service on Lantau.

First-time visitors to Hong Kong are likely to have difficulty working out the exact route a bus will take (the terminus is displayed on the front) and locating appropriate bus stops. Bus routes are constantly changing, and published timetables quickly become outdated so it is better to rely on the HKTA's long experience of explaining the intricacies of the bus system to visitors. A ride on a grubby, unsprung bus during peak hours or on a hot summer's day is not fun, but thanks to bus-only lanes it is an efficient means of getting around. Look for the express buses to Stanley, the Peak and Repulse Bay among other destinations.

Fares range upwards from 60 cents and are charged according to route length. Drop the money into the coin box (the amount is usually displayed by the box) as you get on; no change is given. There are no conductors on board, and you should not rely on any help from the driver in recognising your destination. To signal that you want to get off at the next stop, push the black rubber strip on the ceiling.

Minibuses

Once you work out how to use them, the cream-coloured minibuses with a red stripe, that weave in and out of traffic stopping virtually anywhere, provide a quick, convenient way of getting about. These 14-seater, privately-owned vehicles run mostly on major routes in direct competition with double-decker buses or trams, and thanks to their total disregard for safety and common sense, their drivers cover distances considerably faster than their rivals. The minibus can stop just about anywhere (except in certain restricted zones); hold out your hand to hail a bus, and simply shout at the driver when you want to get out. Choosing the right minibus is sometimes difficult; although the final destination is displayed on the front, the sign is sometimes too small to see until the bus has whizzed past. Fares (shown in the front window and paid when you get off) are a little higher than ordinary buses and fluctuate according to demand, sometimes tripling when it rains or on race days.

Minibuses with a green stripe are known as maxicabs and are under tighter government control than the others. They are designed to serve areas which do not have a full bus service. Fares (usually paid when you get in), frequency and stopping places are all fixed. Many of the most useful routes for tourists have their terminus on either side of the City Hall in Central.

There are no published lists of minibus routes, but the HKTA has details.

Trains

Hong Kong has only one railway line — a section of the old Canton–Kowloon Railway which first opened in 1911. The line has seen grander days, when it formed the last leg of the London–Hong Kong run terminating in a splendid granite and red brick railway station of European proportions (only the clock tower remains on the Tsimshatsui waterfront).

But the fully electrified railway line is certainly well used today. Electrification and modernization of the railway was completed in July 1983; double-tracked, streamlined high-speed cars with a passenger capacity of 775 each are now in operation. Trains run from Kowloon between 6.39 am and 11.21 pm and from Lowu from 6 am to 11.15 pm (7.19 pm is the last train transit to China). Check with the HKTA or at the station for up-to-date timetable information. Tickets have to be bought at the station prior to departure. Stored value tickets are available and they can be used on the MTR as well as KCR routes.

Starting from the new Kowloon station at Hunghom (right beside the cross-harbour tunnel) trains take around 33 minutes to reach Sheung Shui, stopping on the way at Mongkok, Shatin, the Chinese University, Tai Po Kau, Tai Po and Fanling — an interesting journey with picturesque views across Tolo Harbour and glimpses of New Territories rural life. If you have the appropriate travel documents for China, you can stay on the train until the final stop at the border, where Canton-bound passengers climb down and walk across Lowu Bridge into China. There are also four direct express trains a day between Kowloon and Canton. Special trains for Shatin racecourse run on race days.

Avoid trains during the statutory holiday breaks, such as Chinese New Year and Easter, when thousands of people visit friends and

relations in China, or on sunny Sundays when campers, walkers and barbecuers swarm to the New Territories.

Rickshaws

A rickshaw in the traffic chaos of Central or Tsimshatsui looks as incongruous as it would in New York or London. Nevertheless, a few old rickshaw operators lurk by the Star Ferry concourses on both sides of the harbour seeking out tourist business. They will happily pose for pictures and bargain vehemently for a large fee afterwards. No new licences have been issued in many years, and in time the remaining 12 rickshaws will become as extinct as the sedan chairs they themselves supplanted.

The Peak Tram

Hong Kong's famous funicular railway, the Peak Tram, is much more than just the quickest way to ride up the Island's highest mountain — it is one of the most thrilling journeys you can make in the territory.

The tram rises seemingly vertically (the incline is in fact 45 degrees) from the mass of Central's highrise blocks, reaching Victoria Peak a thousand feet higher in around eight minutes. Views are magnificent — across Victoria Harbour to Kowloon and the distant hills of China, and down along the northern strip of Hong Kong Island to Wanchai and Causeway Bay.

Designed by a Scot with experience in Scottish Highland railways, and opened in 1888, the Peak Tramway retains a solid late Victorian aura, with green cars, smooth mahogany slatted wooden seats and mid-way tram stations not unlike miniature versions of British Rail branchline stations. Those apprehensive about the gradient (the steepest in the world it is said), the system's age, or the slight bounce at mid-way stops should be comforted by the tram's perfect safety record.

Tickets cost HK$10 return and service is continuous from 6 am until midnight. It is worth making the trip by day and by night to enjoy the very different, but equally breath-taking views. Try to schedule enough time to walk around the almost level path around Mount Austin. Take a leaf out of the commercial tour operators' book and consider making your downward journey by road — double deckers, minibuses and taxis are all available at the upper terminus. A free bus runs every 20 minutes from the Star Ferry, via Central MTR station, to the Tram's lower terminus in St John's Building, on the edge of Central, a little way up Garden Road opposite the U.S. Consulate.

The tram is far more than a tourist attraction, as the numbers of pinstriped commuters, schoolchildren and shoppers testify, but on Sundays and public holidays you can expect long queues of sightseers and locals, as well as tourists.

Trams

Despite the seeming perpetual redevelopment of the urban areas, Hong Kong's tram system, which was first set up in 1904, has not only miraculously survived, but is thriving.

The distinctive old green double-decker trams rattle along the north side of Hong Kong Island from Kennedy Town through Central to Causeway Bay, North Point and Shaukeiwan, with a single branchline to Happy Valley. They are not for anyone in a hurry, but if you have a window seat on top and there is a breeze to relieve summer heat, this is a pleasant way to get a bird's eye view of some of the liveliest parts of town.

You enter at the back of the tram, making your way forward (no easy task if it is crowded) and paying as you exit at the front. The fare is a flat 60 cents. The final destination of the tram is marked on the front (not all go as far as Shaukeiwan to the east or Kennedy Town to the west). If you are heading towards Causeway Bay or further east, make sure you do not get on a tram that will branch off at Happy Valley. A number of replicas of the earliest trams are available for private hire. A superb red and gold tram with brass trimmings and an upstairs open balcony makes twice-daily *Dim Sum* Tours, 11.15 am to 1.15 pm and 2.15 pm to 4.15 pm. Tickets are price HK$80 (children $60) and can be bought at Star Ferry piers or through travel agents. Telephone 3-669878 or 3-7318483 for further details.

The Mass Transit Railway (MTR)

Hong Kong's latest major engineering triumph, the MTR, has revolutionized transport between Hong Kong Island and Kowloon, and along the northern face of Hong Kong Island. The first 15.5 kilometres (9.7 miles) of underground line were opened in February 1980, stretching from Kwun Tong in east Kowloon, down Nathan Road and under the harbour to Central.

This is the world's first underground rail system to be totally air-conditioned; it also has the world's largest station (in Central).

The system copes with 1.6 million journeys a day. Each vast smooth-gliding carriage seats only 48 (on slippery stainless steel), but there is room for more than 300 to stand.

You need small change to buy your plastic, credit-card-sized, magnetically-encoded tickets from machines. The tickets are slotted through the entrance turnstile and later devoured by an exit turnstile when the journey is over. Look on the concourse walls for directions to the most convenient exit; stations tend to have several, some of them considerable distances apart. If you plan to make more than a few journeys by MTR, consider investing in a stored-value card to avoid the recurring problem of insufficient change. These are sold in denominations from HK$15 to HK$200 at kiosks inside the station concourses.

A 10.4-kilometre (6.5-mile) link from Tsuen Wan in West Kowloon was completed in 1984. The Island Line, along Hong Kong Island's northern shore, links Chai Wan and Sheung Wan and comprises 14 stations. It was completed in 1986.

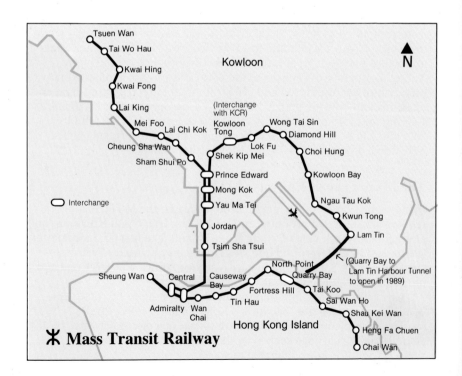

Food in Hong Kong

by Harry Rolnick

With more than 95 percent of Hong Kong's people originally from the bordering province of Kwangtung (Canton), it is hardly surprising that the overwhelming majority of the Territory's restaurants should be devoted to Cantonese cuisine. Fortunately, just as France could be called the apex of European cuisine, so Cantonese has long been regarded as the most subtle, multifarious, ingenious and interesting of all the Chinese cuisines.

Equally fortunately, the Cantonese are not quite so prejudiced against other cuisines as, say, the metropolitan Parisian might be against 'inferior' foreign dishes. The Cantonese diner may habituate himself to his native fare, but he has nothing against a spicy night out with some Sichuan food; he loves his oily, warming Shanghai dishes during the wintertime; and for those very special occasions, he'll impress everybody by taking them to a Peking banquet, the centre of which is Peking duck or Hangchow beggar's chicken.

The third part of Hong Kong's culinary good fortune is that the expatriates, predominantly from the U.S., Scotland and England, have eschewed their own provinciality, and are willing to indulge in foods from all over Asia — if only as a reminder that much of these exotic foods came from one-time colonies. In addition the burgeoning tourist trade over the past decade has meant that many European restaurants of high quality have made their mark here, to the benefit of all.

The China Syndrome

For a casual visitor, the words 'Chinese restaurant' might suffice, but to those who truly enjoy their eating, the words mean practically nothing. Outside of the major differences in the regions, there are so many different types of restaurants, so many seasonal imperatives and so many different ways of eating, that the syndrome of Chinese food is virtually infinite.

The most informal and least expensive eateries are the street restaurants or noodle stalls. The most popular for tourists are in the **'Poor Man's Nightclub'** where hundreds of stalls are set up adjacent to the Macau Ferry Pier. Naturally there are no written menus. You walk from stall to stall pointing to what looks good, then sit down on a rickety chair by a more rickety table. Everything will be delivered to your table, and somehow the bill will be totted up by the various entrepreneurs, usually with faultless accuracy.

The variety can extend from ox, pig and cow offal to the freshest seafood (the latter surprisingly expensive for such an important fishing town). There are a dozen different kinds of noodles, and noodle soup with wonton or meats and vegetables. And of course nearly everything is accompanied by rice. It is usually good fun, if you do not mind being stared at during the meal.

Up a few grades are the morning *dim sum* restaurants. In fact almost every Cantonese-style restaurant serves *dim sum* from 6 am through lunch. The food is not so much a meal as a very happy ritual of almost classical Chinese leisure: sitting, drinking the most sublime of drinks, tea, and eating a variety of dishes without ever hurrying. *Dim sum* has two distinct advantages. First, the food is usually on display, passed around in little bamboo baskets, so you do not need to understand a word of Cantonese to order. Simply point a finger, and the basket is placed on the table. You do not need to worry about a written bill. At the end of the meal, the baskets are added up, and the price is paid; invariably, it is very reasonable too. The other advantage is that these little Chinese *hors d'oeuvres* — literally 'little hearts' — are delicious.

Third up the scale are the ordinary meals in Chinese restaurants. Except for very small restaurants (equivalent to indoor noodle stalls) and the monstrous ones in far-out sections of Hong Kong where foreigners rarely wander, nearly all restaurants have English-language menus. Unfortunately, even with lists of up to 500 different dishes, some of the best are not even mentioned. Your best bets in this case are: a) to enlist a friendly waiter to help you; b) go with some Chinese friends; c) if you spot something good on another table, do not hesitate to ask what it is.

A point to remember is that Chinese dishes here are very different from those in your own country. The great pride of Cantonese food is that it is always fresh. And as the greens in London or seafood in San Francisco are different from the *choi* or shrimp of Hong Kong, the ingredients and tastes will be unlike those you know back home.

The most important thing in Chinese dining is ordering. Remember that democracy at a large Chinese party is unheard of. The host will take the menu and decide what others will have. After checking food prejudices (that is, whether eel or pork or fish lips is acceptable to all), the leader will begin ordering. A basic plan is to start with a cold dish, then order one beef, one pork, one vegetable, one seafood or fish, one soup, some noodles or fried rice. Traditionally, a single plate should be ordered for each member of the party, plus one more. The waiter will determine what size platter to bring: for up to four, a small serving will do, up to nine or ten a medium-sized dish, and after that, a large portion.

As Chinese food has been an 'in' thing in most occidental capitals, most visitors have some idea of the differences between the regions, but here is a rundown:

Cantonese The best Cantonese food in the world is in Hong Kong. The preparations are traditional (as they are in Canton itself), but the ingredients come not only from China but Hong Kong (the New Territories was once called 'The Emperor's Rice Bowl' for the richness of its produce) and the rest of the world. The emphasis is on fast cooking to bring dishes to the apex of their natural taste and colour. No greasy dishes are ever served. If they are not fast-fried in a minimum of oil, they are steamed or broiled. Few spices are used but there are many sauces. The Guangdong coast supplies remarkable seafood, as well as an abundance of fowl, meat and vegetables, including an endless variety of mushrooms. Truly this is the world's greatest cuisine — as even the Parisian practitioners of nouvelle cuisine are happy to point out.

Pekingese The arid desert of northern China has little in the way of natural ingredients, unlike tropical and sub-tropical Canton. But as Peking has been the capital of China since early times, the best produce was sent up to the Emperor's palaces, and some fine recipes were devised. The best known dish is Peking duck, but the Mongolian hotpot is popular, as are lamb and mutton dishes, especially during winter. You rarely eat rice with this food. Instead, ask for some dumplings (perhaps half steamed, half fried). You should wind up the meal with noodles and vegetables.

Sichuanese This is the spiciest of all Chinese food. Garlic, pepper, fennel, coriander and star anise all grow in Sichuan province and are added liberally to the steamed, simmered, smoked dishes. These include excellent seafood, superb fowl and eggplant, as well as an intriguing sour-and-hot soup to finish off the meal. Be prepared for a *lot* of garlic.

Shanghainese This is a bit greasier than some, a little sweeter, and the dishes are fried for a long time in sesame or soy sauce. The seafood — especially eel and winter crab — is good, and the portions are enormous. The dumplings are tasty, and the little shrimp with pieces of garlic and pepper are excellent. Many of the dishes come from other provinces, befitting Shanghai's status as the largest port in China and its most cosmopolitan city.

Hakka and **Chiu Chow** Both of these cuisines come from the south of China, and neither is very popular outside the Far East. But Chiu Chow food is gutsy, with thick sharks' fin soup, goose doused in soy sauce, excellent seafood and all kinds of birds' nest dishes. Usually these restaurants do not close until 3 am. Hakka food comes from a nomadic people who must preserve their food. Consequently, many of the best dishes are salted down (like salt chicken or salted cabbage) and are not terribly appealing, save that the mixed vegetable dish, *lo han*, is probably the best of all vegetable dishes.

In the top grade of all Chinese food is the Man Han Banquet — and should you be so lucky as to be invited to one of these rare occasions, do go. A traditional banquet is not simply one dinner — it consists of at least three days of dining. And of the 100-odd dishes, not a single one is duplicated.

To quote from one of the Chinese sages: 'Let there be plenty of food and plenty of clothing, and propriety and righteousness will flourish.'

The Tables of Asia

With immigrants from all parts of Asia, and with a European population always on the look-out for different foods, it is little wonder that Hong Kong can serve dishes from all over the Orient. Granted, some of the restaurants aren't always the cleanest (one thinks immediately of the Indian restaurants in Chungking Mansions, on Kowloon side), but for the most part health laws are so stringent that you can eat safely.

For the record, countries represented include India (mainly North India, but with a few Madras dishes served in Chungking Mansions), Pakistan (virtually the same as North India), Indonesia (spicy, with coconut milk and *sambal* hot sauces), Malaysia (virtually the same as Indonesia, but with less variety, as the restaurants are run by Chinese), Japan, Korea (very spicy, marvellous barbecued beef), Thailand (spicy curries, with a plethora of coriander, fine hot salads, soups filled with tangy lemon grass, and good curries), and Vietnam (where the food is mild except for the vinegar and includes dewy-fresh greens, mint, lettuce, etc).

Food from the Long-nosed Barbarians

Traditionally, European food was as much an anathema to the Chinese as were Europeans themselves. In multi-national Hong Kong, this has obviously changed — and rare is the young Chinese who does not indulge at fast food shops like McDonald's.

Every hotel has its restaurants, and first-class hotels nearly always have European managers. Prices are faily reasonable for cuisine, fairly unreasonable for wines. (Hong Kong is duty-free in everything except cigarettes and liquor.) The best bargains are the buffets. The Hilton, Furama, Peninsula, and The Hongkong Hotel all have superb buffets, at prices from HK$80 to HK$100.

At private restaurants, the *prix fixe* lunches are about one-third the price of *à la carte* meals. Gaddi's, Chesa and Au Trou Normand are usually expensive, so these set lunches fall into the bargain class.

Outside of the hotels, a number of 'ethnic' restaurants are around: little Mexican café's, pizzerias, a few delicatessens, some Hungarian food, and around Wanchai one can have very inexpensive ordinary European dishes.

At first-class restaurants outside the hotels, included in the list on page 000, prices are usually a little less, though wine is still high. And at these places, you can hobnob with residents of Hong Kong, not simply other travellers.

When dining out in Hong Kong the main rule is to be adventurous about trying new dishes and restaurants off the beaten path. If Hong Kong people are handsome, healthy, hard-working and hearty, they are the prime heirs of the dictum offered by Confucius, back in the fifth century BC. 'Great food,' he said, 'is the first happiness.'

Farmers still practise centuries-old watering techniques

Shopping in Hong Kong

It is no exaggeration to say that Hong Kong's tourist industry was built on the attraction of its shopping, which accounts for 52 per cent of all visitors' expenditure, or about HK$2,857 million in 1987. Almost all goods are imported duty free, which in theory makes them cheaper than anywhere else, including their country of origin. In fact, astronomical rents in central shopping districts have forced some prices up and offset this advantage. Many store owners have moved a few blocks from Central and Nathan Road, and a wise shopper should follow them.

Fortunately, more and more goods are made in Hong Kong, and there is a growing market in clothes, electronics, toys and optical equipment designed for export but available in local shops at prices far below the imported equivalents. Besides tourists, shopkeepers can depend on a healthy domestic market of six million keen consumers.

Hong Kong's skilled, industrious workers have long since left their sweatshops but they are still willing to labour at all hours to sew a suit, carve a camphorwood chest or fashion a piece of jewellery to order. This is the basic reason why Hong Kong is still unrivalled as the place for custom-made items of excellent quality at very reasonable prices.

In recent years, Hong Kong has benefited as the prime showcase for goods made in China. Ranging from garments to bicycles, medicine to musical instruments, these products are far more abundant and invariably cheaper than in stores in China itself and so many souvenirs from the People's Republic are actually bought in Hong Kong instead.

Any shopping expedition in Hong Kong can be daunting. No one has counted the number of shops, but 1,300 of them are members of the HKTA. These are to be recommended as the HKTA undertakes to deal with any complaints from customers and stores can be struck off for dishonest dealings. (Watch out for the HKTA junk logo in the window.) The HKTA also helps visitors by listing all their shop members, together with a price guide, in a free booklet *The Official Guide to Eating Out and Services in Hong Kong*, available at any of the association's information offices.

There are three major shopping areas for tourists in Central District. The most expensive is around the super-deluxe arcades of the Landmark building, but walk a few blocks west and the prices tumble. The Golden Mile of Nathan Road and streets leading from it in Tsimshatsui are packed with shops. Here the competition is keen and comparison shopping is well worth while. Probably the lowest prices are found in Causeway Bay, where most of the customers are local residents.

Dedicated shoppers will enjoy exploring the many small stores in these areas. Others might prefer conveniently compact shopping centres, especially when it is hot or raining. The arcades found in many hotels are the most convenient, but remember the rent-price tag connection! For a wide range of shops and very reasonable prices, the best bet is the vast air-conditioned complex of Ocean Terminal and Ocean Centre, adjoining The Hongkong Hotel. Or why not take the MTR out to Tai Koo and join the locals on their own bargain hunt through Tai Koo Shing's magnificent Cityplaza?

In addition, there are plenty of department stores. For first-class imports visit Lane Crawford or Shui Hing; for Japanese products Daimaru, Sogo, Matsuzakaya, Isetan, Mitsukoshi and most recently Uny have opened branches in Hong Kong; and for a wealth of goods made in China, go to one of the Yue Hwa stores in Kowloon or China Products in Causeway Bay.

In these stores prices are fixed but in other shops and at street stalls bargaining is expected. In fact customers are regularly offered a 'special price' or a discount of 10 per cent and some persistence will usually result in a further reduction. Be warned, however, that this only applies when you use cash. Most shops accept the major credit cards, but their attitude tends to be that the handling charge cancels out any discount. This is particularly true at sale time — whether the 'sale' price is a bona fide reduction or not — and you will save time and temper by announcing at the start of the transaction how you intend to pay. Also, shops will often take foreign currency in payment, but do not expect to get the best exchange rate.

Finally, some basic pointers that everyone practises back home but which can slip from even the hardiest shopper's repertoire once the pace and glitter of Hong Kong begins to work its spell. The first rule is self-explanatory and concerns comparison shopping: whatever the bargain, however honey-tongued the sales clerk, scout around, check and compare until you have proved to your own satisfaction that the price is fair.

When it comes to buying cameras, videos and watches, remember that though it may be fun to pick up the occasional cheap clone of the expensive real thing back home, it is unfair to expect an inappropriately robust performance. Electrical items should be checked for domestic compatibility of voltage, frequency or broadcasting system (VHS, Betamax, PAL, SECAM, etc.) and detailed, legible receipts with accompanying guarantees are a must. Never buy anything unseen, and if you must leave a deposit do not go above 10 per cent. (Lest this makes Hong Kong sound a labyrinth of uncertainty, the HKTA produces a range of reassuring — and free — booklets of advice including a *Shopping Guide to Video Equipment* naming sole agents and recommended HKTA retailers.)

Except for department stores and shops in high-class arcades, which open six days a week from 10 am to 6 pm, most shops are open every day from 10 am to 10 pm.

Garments and Fabrics

Every kind of ready-made garment is available in Hong Kong from European high fashion to Chinese-made padded jackets, to overruns of designer jeans and sportswear. In Central District, a browse through the Landmark complex, Swire House and Prince's Building provides an interesting comparison with the shopping arcades of the top hotels such as Mandarin Oriental, the Peninsula and the Regent. These tend to be centres for couturier boutiques, so if your money matches your taste, you could do a lot worse than to make for the long-established Joyce Boutique in the Landmark with its excellent selection of designer fashion garments from Europe. Nor should you bypass the very talented local designers such as Lily Chao, Joseph Ho or Eddie Lau or the Japanese boutiques such as Issey Miyake, Matsuda and Paris-based Kenzo. Equally pricey, albeit ever-popular, are the exquisitely made *cheong sam* and sequined and beaded gowns and jackets from Jenny Lewis. Devotees of Diane Freis are more than adequately cared for with shops throughout Central and Tsimshatsui selling her dresses, separates and knitwear. Furs made from Siberian or Chinese skins also are good buys, especially when made to order; one of the most reliable and long-established dealers in this field is

Siberian Furs with branches on Des Voeux Road in Central as well as
Chatham Road, Tsimshatsui. If you are searching in the moderately
priced ranges of silk blouses, dressing gowns and padded jackets, you
should make straight for the amply stocked Chinese department stores.

Those on the island side searching out fashion sportswear of the
calibre of Giordano, Fila, Esprit and Benetton should head for
Causeway Bay and the streets surrounding the Lee Gardens and
Excelsior Hotels; those in Kowloon will find them all along Nathan
Road. Crocodile (Crocokid label) and The Children Clothing
Company also have outlets throughout Hong Kong and Kowloon. For
overruns of designer jeans and much, much more, make haste to the
south side of the island and the world-famous Stanley Market — but
do not bank too seriously on those I. Magnin or Lord & Taylor labels!
Still in Stanley, the long-established Fudo Jeans also has a branch in
Spring Garden Lane, Wanchai. For those less label-conscious, the
markets in Jardine's Crescent (Causeway Bay) or Granville and
Haiphong Roads (Tsimshatsui) should prove fruitful but always check
for dyeing faults, tears and crooked seams. The same goes for
children's clothes and the ever-popular overruns that can be found in
the markets.

Factory outlets are best known for their silk and knit dresses,
separates and accessories and, again, those ubiquitous designer
overruns. They are located in both Central and Kowloon and
particularly at Kaiser Estate, Phases I and II, in Hung Hom. Those
with outlets on both sides of the harbour include Camberley
Enterprises (for Anne Klein II), Four Seasons, Shopper's World and
Vica Moda. Browsers in Central should not miss out the cavernous
Pedder Building which has been known to yield more than a few
pleasant surprises. For the latest and reliable details, look no further
than the HKTA's booklet on factory outlets in Hong Kong.

Hong Kong is famed for its custom-made clothing and, given the
skill of local tailors and the availability of reasonably priced fabrics,
from Chinese silk brocade to British woollens, it is the ideal place to
have clothes made to measure. Good buys in silk and to a lesser
degree wool and corduroy can be found at most Chinese department
stores. Excellent bargains are also to be found in Wing On Street
(otherwise known as 'Cloth Alley') and the surrounding 'lanes' snaking
off Queen's Road Central and Des Voeux Road.

As for tailors, they are absolutely everywhere. In side-streets and
shopping blocks and perched patiently in the arcades of grand hotels,
they tend to sell the pricier wools and mixed fabrics from Britain and
Italy. Allow time for two or three fittings or give the tailor a garment
to copy. Many satisfied customers continue to order clothes long after
they return home, usually with excellent results.

Shoes

Ready-made shoes are also available in Hong Kong but usually in the smaller sizes. Stores specializing in custom-made shoes and boots for foreigners tend to be those like Mayer Shoes in the Mandarin Hotel and Lily Shoes in the Peninsula Hotel, neither of which is cheap. Moderately priced, locally made shoes are found along Wongneichong Road in Happy Valley where there is a whole string of shops. For the sporting variety, try Stanley Market or the side-streets off Nathan Road in Tsimshatsui.

Jewellery

Gold is imported duty-free and is relatively cheap. At most jewellery stores the day's price of gold is displayed (so many dollars per *tael*, the equivalent of 1.2 troy ounces). Even if you only count the side alleys leading from Nathan Road, Hong Kong is home to literally thousands of jewellery stores and each one follows its own sales policy and bargaining technique. The best you can do is to stick to accredited dealers such as members of the HKTA whose distinctive junk logo can be seen on windows and doorways. All kinds of precious and semi-precious stones can be bought, set or unset, and expert craftsmen can follow individual designs to give you a unique ring or necklace. Hong Kong is one of the world's major diamond traders and, by and large, dealers are honest and helpful. If in doubt, call the Diamond Importers Association at 5-235497 or the Gemmological Association of Hong Kong at 3-666006. At the same time, with all the advice available on where and from whom to buy, it is worth remembering that the only realistic attitude in purchasing is that you are not acquiring an investment but buying a gem you cannot live without. It is rare to recoup your money except in a private sale.

Jade is considered a stone from heaven by the Chinese and a valued talisman. As a result Hong Kong has the world's best selection of jade but prices tend to be high. For cheap pieces visit the Jade Market (see Kowloon), for more expensive jewellery and figurines be sure you know what you are doing. Jade comes not only in various shades of green and opaqueness but also in white, yellow, orange and lavender and, although it boils down to a question of personal taste, most lovers of jade regard the best pieces as possessing all these colours.

Pearls come in an enormous range and Hong Kong stocks them all, from the cultured and evenly matched to the baroque, fresh-water version and natural black. Colours can vary from cream to a distinct pink and, again, although both this and the shape are down to personal

preference, the price rests on size and quality.

Many stores sell ivory objects and Hong Kong is one of the biggest importers of tusks (many smuggled in), but do your bit for conservation and ignore these pieces.

If chunky handcrafted silver is your fancy, take a watchful walk along Hollywood Road and Cat Street (above Queen's Road Central) or visit the Chinese department stores where they also sell beaded semi-precious and porcelain necklaces. China Arts & Crafts features local designer Kai Yin Lo's less expensive line in necklaces and earrings made of amethyst, turquoise, jade and quartz. Her shops in the Mandarin and Peninsula Hotels are much pricier.

Cameras and Optical Equipment

Hundreds of stores throughout Hong Kong and on both sides of the harbour sell a bewildering selection of the very latest in photographic equipment. Nowadays you are as likely to find what you want in Hankow Road or the Ocean Centre complex as Nathan Road or anywhere around Causeway Bay. Sales staff are usually well informed and helpful. Prices tend to be 10 per cent off list, and you can ask to see the list. A useful booklet is on sale here, titled *How to Avoid Getting Ripped-Off in Hong Kong Buying Cameras and Photo Accessories* by James Morgan. Hong Kong-produced binoculars are among the best in the world.

Watches and Clocks

Hong Kong is the world's largest manufacturer of watches, mostly of the cheaper reliable variety. For the best prices try the shops along Queen's Road Central or the side streets of Kowloon, and always bargain. When buying an expensive brand make sure you get the manufacturer's guarantee and beware of incredible discounts; there have been cases of inferior workings behind the Rolex or Omega faces. For a wide selection of time pieces of every description try City Chain Stores whose numerous branches are evenly scattered on both sides of the harbour.

A lot of fun can be had picking out one or two *bijoux* items such as the startlingly convincing line in 'Rock' watches.

Electronics and Sound Equipment

Hong Kong is an Aladdin's Cave for stereo enthusiasts and kids of all ages. Here you will find all of the remarkable 'toys' of the new electronic age, from complex sound systems to tiny calculators which do everything except make your morning tea, and pocket-sized electronic games. The dealers like to keep their stock moving, so it pays to bargain.

Only four years old and the first of its kind in Asia, the Asia Computer Plaza in Silvercord Building, Canton Road, Tsimshatsui is a hacker's dream. Under one roof it houses every type and size of computer as well as stocklists of the more elusive peripherals and software, and there are even exhibitions and regular displays and seminars to keep the consumer fully up to date. Particularly useful is ACP's own switchboard at 3-7346111. It can connect you to an information centre from which you can either collect up-to-date product listings or be transferred on to any outlet you choose.

The usual *caveat* about not leaving deposits is particularly relevant to the electronics industry where smaller merchants have been known to shut up shop and disappear literally overnight.

Antiques and Handicrafts

You are not likely to find a Ming vase for HK$10 but there are still bargains in Chinese antiques to be uncovered along Hong Kong's Hollywood Road, in the 'Cat Street' area (now sadly diminished by redevelopment, although Cat Street Galleries on Lok Ku Road is well worth an exploration). Wyndham Street and Hollywood Road are good hunting grounds for those low Japanese side tables, Filipino *dulangs* (ideal as coffee tables) and Korean chests which, in the case of the latter, can also be bought in the Ocean City/Harbour City complex. There are also 'instant' antiques, faithful reproductions of classic pieces which nevertheless show the enduring skill of Chinese craftsmen. For absolutely genuine antiques, at appropriate prices, there is Charlotte Horstmann and Chinese Arts & Crafts. The latter stores also sell beautiful handicrafts such as painted scrolls, lacquered fans, paper cut-outs, embroidered table linen and many other excellent gifts and souvenirs. Other names to bear in mind in this field, especially for handicrafts, are the Banyan Tree, Amazing Grace and Mountain Folkcraft, all of which have shops in Central and Tsimshatsui and are good for anything from cushion covers, baskets and batik jackets, to masks and wooden puppets.

Furniture and Carpets

Craftsmen have kept up the tradition of great woodwork in Hong Kong, and custom-made chests, side-boards, tables and chairs —

carved, inlaid with mother-of-pearl or gilded — are spectacular buys. For locally made rattan furniture, Queen's Road East is the best area and most shops have an impressive range of catalogues from which to order. For rosewood and blackwood furniture, Queen's Road East, Hollywood Road and the Ocean Centre complex are probably the most accessible areas. Luk's Furniture in Aberdeen has an extensive selection, and all of these are clued up on the various shipping details. Special stores sell Persian, Indian and Chinese carpets, both antique and modern, as well as locally made Tai Ping ones (see New Territories, page 141). Indian and Persian carpets are best tracked down along Wyndham Street and Hollywood Road, and Chinese carpets can be found in any large Chinese department store as well as in many shops in Ocean Terminal.

Miscellaneous

Hong Kong probably has the best selection of luggage, briefcases and other carrying bags anywhere. They range from very inexpensive canvas suitcases to custom-made bags of the finest leather. For the former try shopping in alleys and the lanes such as Li Yuen Street or any of the Chinese department stores; for the latter visit Gucci and Louis Vuitton in the Landmark, Trussardi in the Peninsula Hotel's shopping arcade or any reputable leather goods shop.

Hong Kong-made spectacles are excellent and the standard of opticians very high, so it might be worth your while to get your glasses here. Eye tests are free, but allow yourself time to wear in your spectacles in case of unforeseen difficulties.

For porcelain and china, the first places to make for are the Chinese department stores with their comprehensive range of stools, umbrella stands, vases and traditionally patterned Chinese crockery. Also fertile ground is Hollywood Road and along Cat Street, and there is a particularly extensive selection in Cat Street Galleries itself.

No one makes more toys than Hong Kong but they are mostly for export, which leaves the charming local variety such as the cloth and wooden dolls one finds in handicraft shops or Chinese department stores. For the real thing, however, Toys 'Я' Us operates a vast emporium in Ocean Terminal that is piled high with every conceivable plaything and childhood treasure.

As a final indication of the range of custom-made items available in this market where all things are possible, you can have a name chop made with your name in Chinese characters for a few dollars, or you can order a specially created yacht or pleasure junk for a few hundred thousand.

Arts and Entertainment

Until recent years Hong Kong's cultural development has been hampered by the lack of good venues for concerts, ballet, theatre, and exhibitions. Even today every year sees a number of first class international musicians or other artists unable to perform here simply because no suitable hall is available. By contrast, neighbouring Japan has thousands of concert halls throughout the country. Hong Kong certainly cannot compete with what is available in cities like Tokyo and Osaka, but there are some outstanding performances, and subsidies hold ticket prices far below what you would have to pay in most North American, European or Japanese cities.

Exhibition and gallery space is still limited, although in the past few years a number of small private galleries have opened, mainly specialising in prints and pottery. The visual arts as a whole still tend to have Cinderella status in Hong Kong — the territory has no art school and local artists have had to go elsewhere for training, if they could afford it, or study privately and at evening classes. In the face of such difficulties the only surprise is that Hong Kong does in fact have a number of remarkably gifted artists, whose work has won widespread international recognition.

From time to time there are superb exhibitions, by local artists and also by Chinese masters from the mainland or artists around the world whose work is brought in by a government or private agency. So if you are interested in the visual arts, it is worth dropping in to any exhibition you see listed, even if it sounds commercial.

The past decade has seen a burgeoning of more or less full-time professional dance and vernacular theatre companies in Hong Kong, using local choreographers and playwrights. Standards can be unpredictable, but Hong Kong's cultural scene is still worth a look.

Hong Kong's home of culture for long was the City Hall, next to the Star Ferry terminal on Hong Kong Island. Rather than municipal offices, as its name suggests, this is a cluster of concert hall, theatre and libraries, plus exhibition space. About 10 minutes walk further east stands the futuristic-looking Academy for the Performing Arts (APA), with skeletal flying buttresses, purple carpets and all, plus a very fine theatre and concert hall. Almost opposite is the Hong Kong Arts Centre, which has a small theatre, plus two venues for experimental performances and exhibition space.

In the New Territories, Hong Kong's 'satellite cities' and 'new towns' — Tuen Mun, Tsuen Wan, Sha Tin and Tai Po among others — have their own town halls, incorporating excellent auditoria where some of the world's finest orchestras and soloists have appeared. Hong

Kong's two multi-purpose venues — the Coliseum, alongside the Hunghom Railway Station, and the Queen Elizabeth Stadium in Wanchai — have been used by everyone from visiting gymnastic and ping-pong teams to the London Royal Ballet and Holiday on Ice.

A number of theatres have been purpose built for Chinese opera, the oldest and most elegant being the Lee in Causeway Bay, which serves as a regular cinema when there is no live production. The Sunbeam in King's Road, North Point has a large enough stage to take acrobatic and other performing troupes from China as well as opera; it, too, is used as a cinema for much of the year.

Perhaps the most interesting forum for the arts is the Fringe Club, a steep 100 yards or so up Wyndham Street in Central. Standards of performances and exhibitions vary greatly, but the umber and cream painted building dates back to 1924 and is well worth a visit. It was formerly an ice house in pre-refrigeration times and so is a real part of Hong Kong's history.

Local cultural life promises to come of age early in 1989 with the completion of the many on-stage venues in the inelegantly named Cultural Complex on the Tsimshatsui waterfront, next to the Kowloon Star Ferry terminal.

Despite the amount of arts activity, Hong Kong has no central clearing point for information, and the biggest challenge is to find out what is available. English-language radio stations, newspapers and other publications feature more or less complete listings of events, while advertisements can give some notion of what is coming in the near future. The hardest network to hook into is the most interesting — the traditional Chinese performances.

Tickets for a variety of productions are normally available through two main 'chains': URBTIX and Tom Lee sell tickets for all Urban Council-managed venues plus the APA and Arts Centre; TICKET-MATE sells tickets for jetfoils and hydrofoils to Macau plus performances in the Arts Centre and some other locations.

Ask the HKTA if there are any scheduled performances of Chinese music, folk dance, magic or acrobatics. The Landmark in Central, Citiplaza in Tai Koo Shing and the Ocean Terminal in Tsimshatsui, Kowloon, all have free shows from time to time.

Look at listings to find performances of Chinese instrumental music. Hong Kong's professional Chinese Orchestra and a number of remarkably gifted solo players give regular concerts. The instruments are exotic to look at and generally the sounds are mellow and tuneful, if a little bewildering to the unaccustomed ear. Public playgrounds and other informal settings are sometimes used to supplement more formal venues.

Arts Festivals

Three more or less annual festivals may be of interest to visitors. Although the best seats tend to be snapped up weeks in advance by residents, returns may be available just before a performance begins.

The **Festival of Asian Arts**, held most years around October, is a gathering of dance, music and visual presentations of varying quality from most countries in the region. Although some items are pedestrian or worse, the festival can provide unique opportunities to enjoy some fascinating dance and music.

In January–February, the **Hong Kong Arts Festival** provides a concentrated four weeks of largely Western imported arts: music, theatre, mime, jazz and dance, with some productions from the People's Republic of China.

Hong Kong's **International Film Festival** is usually held in the spring. Tickets sell out well in advance of this unstructured feast for residents. But, apart from the Asian Cinema section, it is likely to be dismissed as less than exciting by visitors accustomed to the rich fare of Western cinematic centres.

Cinema

International though Hong Kong may be in many respects, its cinematic offerings can be second-rate. Apart from the latest Hollywood award-winning films, little of the best of American or European cinema finds its way onto the commercial circuit. And when it does, it may well be cut, either by the censors or by a theatre manager whose main concern is fitting the film into a neat two-hour programme slot.

Hong Kong possesses a number of commercial cinemas that could claim a luxury label: the plush Palace in the World Trade Centre, and Columbia Classics in Great Eagle Centre. For the rest, be prepared for noisy comings and goings throughout the film, smokers and small children in the audience, and the possibility of distorted sound. Seats are generally inexpensive, ranging upwards from HK$20. For films newly released in Hong Kong tickets should be bought in advance from the cinema box office. And double check that you are going to the film you want: box office failures are taken off overnight.

The showings by two film clubs, Studio One and the Phoenix Cine Club, are for members only. For the general public the Goethe Institute, the Alliance Francaise, the British Council and other bodies run film programmes. Watch for advertisements to find out what is available.

Chinese Opera

Whether it be broadcast, televised or live in a theatre, performed by people or by puppets, Chinese opera has a devoted following in Hong Kong. The territory has a number of professional troupes, which include some excellent young performers trained in China. Visiting troupes from different regions of China always are extremely popular. Like Western opera, Chinese opera depends heavily on colour and theatrical effects for its impact. Traditionally scenery was not used beyond a plain wooden chair or table and, as in the Elizabethan theatre, everything else was supplied by the imagination. These days realistic sets are more common, but the performer still dominates the stage. Actors specialise in a certain type of role, or even one particular example of a certain category, which they continue to play throughout their careers. All singing is in a characteristic falsetto voice which takes many years to perfect. Although it may sound harsh, it can still be highly expressive. In the past only men could become actors, but today all roles are unisex, depending on the talent of the individual.

Platform shoes, lofty headdresses, and brilliantly coloured, padded costumes laden with sequins make the actor appear larger than life. Extra-long 'water sleeves' of white silk are attached to basic brocade, to be used to emphasise gestures. The 'orchestral' accompaniment uses gongs and drums to heighten the drama as a significant character moves on or off stage.

Stylized movements make it instantly clear that the hero is in a boat, riding a horse, or in a carriage, in the dark, entering or leaving the house and so on. Costume and make-up also reveal the character's role — hero, villain, adolescent boy, coquette or magistrate. The story will be familiar to the audience, raised on the epics of intrigue and valour, star-crossed love and self-sacrifice that have been woven around China's favourite folk heroes.

Many of the most popular operas have little discernible story, as they are often simply a lengthy elaboration of a single episode from a well-known tale of derring-do, and the newcomer tends to find them static after a short while. Others, like 'The White Snake' or the 'Journey to the West', have such fast-paced action that the eye cannot keep pace with the frenetic whirling, twirling and somersaulting on stage.

Different parts of China developed their own styles of performance, although nowadays many of the distinctions are blurred. Peking opera is still regarded as the purest and most classical form, and a really good performance is an experience to treasure.

China's emperors were reputedly connoisseurs of opera and did much to foster professional troupes. Major festivals and other events

楊紫瓊 領銜主演

監製：
洪金寶
導演：
元奎
聯合主演：
岑建勳
孟　海
徐　克

主演：狄　威
　　　鍾發
　　　田俊
　　　羅芙洛

皇家師姐

YES, MADAM!

D
錦好戲錦德寶

became occasions early on for public performances, and to some extent this continues in modern Hong Kong (see Festivals on page 80). The concept of opera-in-a-theatre is relatively recent and you may be disconcerted to find the audience chatting, eating, drinking tea and soft drinks, seemingly doing anything but paying attention to the stage. Stay long enough and you will become aware of a distinct pattern, interest waxing as the singing becomes more impassioned, or a particularly well-executed series of movements ends in a graceful pose worthy of an Olympic gymnast.

It is not always possible but it certainly helps to have some notion of the story before you go to a performance, as there is rarely even a synopsis in English. If you can, find a brief explanation of the most important stage conventions. Above all, go with an open mind, prepared to enjoy what is still in any form a unique spectacle, incorporating many different art forms in one clashing, blazing, glorious whole.

Parallel to the tradition of human theatre runs the development of various kinds of puppet troupes performing the same repertoire on a small scale.

The Media

Radio and Television Recent figures indicate that 98 percent of the Territory's households have a television. There are four commercial channels, two in English, two in Chinese, which put out mostly mediocre programmes, with the few high spots often aired far into the night. For English language radio programmes, government-financed RTHK puts out Radio 3 (news, light music), Radio 4 (news, current affairs, classical music, some BBC programmes) and Radio 5 (BBC World Service). There is also one English language commercial station and one run by the British Forces Broadcasting Service.

Press The people of Hong Kong are enthusiastic newspaper readers. Of the territory's 72 daily newspapers, only two are in English — the establishment-owned *South China Morning Post* and the more lively *Hongkong Standard*. Publications from around the world are, however, freely available in Hong Kong; the *Asian Wall Street Journal* and the Asian edition of the *International Herald Tribune* both publish in Hong Kong as do the weeklies, the *Far Eastern Economic Review* (widely recognised for its authoritative business and China reporting) and *Asiaweek* (which gives a more Asian perspective to coverage of regional news).

Finding out What's On in Hong Kong

City News is a monthly newspaper containing a full list of performances at the City Hall, sports events organised or sponsored by the Urban Council, and a programme of entertainment on at the Queen Elizabeth Stadium. Free, available in the City Hall.

Arts Centre programme for the month: A leaflet listing all presentations at the Arts Centre. Free, available at the Arts Centre.

Queen Elizabeth Stadium programme for the month: A leaflet listing all sports events, performances and classes taking place at the stadium. Free, available at the stadium box office.

Orient is a weekly newspaper produced by the HKTA. Its 'This Week' column is reasonably comprehensive and one of the few sources for news of Chinese opera performances. Free at hotels and HKTA offices.

Television and radio: On television there are five-minute programmes. 'What's On' on Radio 3 at 8.30 pm is the most comprehensive. ATV and TVB, the two English-language television stations, broadcast similar information, but with changing schedules. Check the newspaper for exact timings.

Box Offices:

City Hall 5-229928 and 5-739595	Open daily 11 am – 9.30 pm
Arts Centre 5-8230230	Open daily 10 am – 8.15 pm
Queen Elizabeth Stadium 5-756793	Opening hours vary with events
Tsuen Wan Town Hall 0-440144	Open 12.30 pm – 9.30 pm

Nightlife

Some people say that Hong Kong's nightlife died with the end of the American involvement in the Vietnam War and the departure of the U.S. servicemen who spent their rest and recreation here; others claim that nothing existed in the first place to compare with the exotic and erotic style of Bangkok and Manila.

No one doubts that Hong Kong's night centres have lost some of the glamour of the 50s and 60s and that the night clubs are restrained compared with their counterparts in Thailand and the Philippines. However, Hong Kong does offer an amazing variety of bars, nightclubs, discos, massage parlours and escort services which range from the sophisticated and grossly over-priced down to the frankly seedy, with a host of choices in between to satisfy an equal diversity of tastes.

The areas of night entertainment best known to visitors are Wanchai and Causeway Bay on Hong Kong Island and Tsimshatsui in Kowloon. Most of Wanchai's activities centre on the bustling grid of crowded streets of which Lockhart Road is the main thoroughfare. Despite the arrival of three-star hotels and the restraining influence of the Arts Centre, the one-man tailor businesses and other ordinary establishments, the glow of neon lights still lends the 'Wanch' a uniquely nostalgic atmosphere.

After all, this was the world of Richard Mason's *Suzie Wong* and it is even said — albeit not by the management — that the eminently respectable Luk Kwok Hotel (now pulled down) was one of the localities where William Holden and Nancy Kwan shot the film. Across the harbour, Hankow and Nathan Road flank the stately Peninsula Hotel as they head north with their many side-streets and dimly-lit alleys where the traders of the night beckon the unwary towards basement bars or the dizzy heights of a penthouse night club. Hong Kong's nightlife is as varied as the names — Pussycat Bar, Mischievous Moments, Pink Lady Night Club, Bottoms Up and, of course, the inevitable Suzie Wong Bar. Not surprisingly, the names do not all live up to the activities inside, and the terms 'nightclub', 'bar' or 'discotheque' are often used indiscriminately to signify no more than a place to have a drink and perhaps dance to live or taped music as topless waitresses and bar girls go about their task of keeping the glasses filled.

Wanchai and Tsimshatsui offer numerous examples of the particularly Asian phenomenon of the hostess club and the rather less elegant girlie bar. They attract tourists and local residents alike; today Japanese tourists seem to be taking the place of the war-weary American servicemen of the late 60s and early 70s.

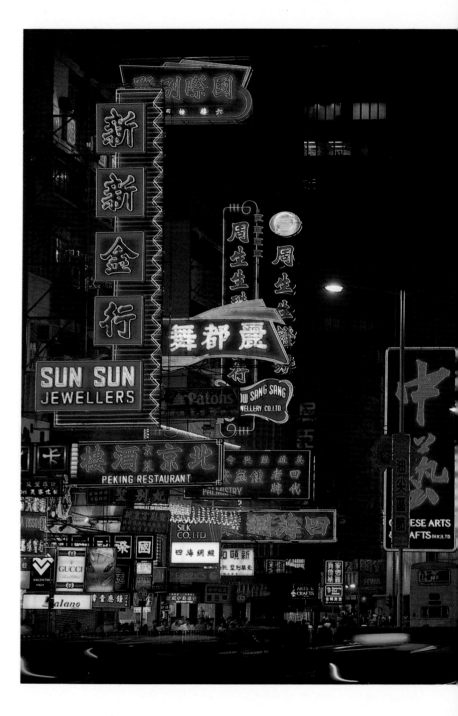

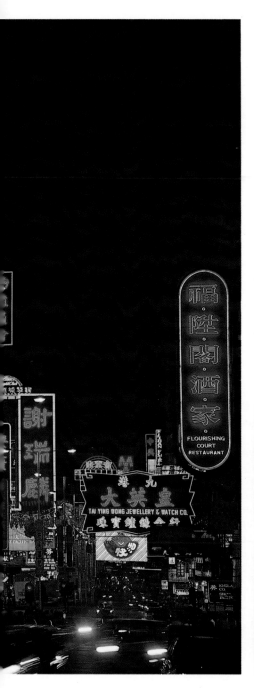

Night lights of the city

As its name implies, the hostess club is strictly for male visitors who require company for an hour or two in a cosy atmosphere with music and a dance-floor, and are willing to pay for it in slots of 15 minutes or so, although the Western visitor may look askance at a dancing partner who fills her time sheet in at the same time. Billing itself as 'the biggest Japanese-style nightclub in the world', **Club Volvo**, Mandarin Plaza, East Tsimshatsui, is the best-known club of its kind in Hong Kong (if not Asia) and occupies 70,000 square feet with 1,100 hostesses and even a mock-up vintage car that traverses the gigantic venue. A luxurious and expensive club is the **Dai-ichi Club**, 1st floor, Harbour View Mansion, 257 Gloucester Road, Causeway Bay; two others are **Club Ginza**, 20 Hankow Road, Kowloon, and the **Club Kokusai**, 81 Nathan Road, Tsimshatsui, one of the oldest of these Japanese-style hostess clubs.

Topless and girlie bars are more difficult to classify and can change owners and personality overnight. Generally the company of the girls inside is not paid for but her drinks are. As with the hostess clubs, the girls are available as escorts outside the establishment but in this case the fee is paid to the bar and an extra fee is negotiated with the escort herself.

One of the best-known and reliable bars in Hong Kong is **Bottoms Up** in the basement of 14−16 Hankow Road, Tsimshatsui. This was Hong Kong's first topless bar and is a favourite with locals and tourists alike — possibly because, as the general manager says, 'We don't hustle our customers, we pamper them.' Topless barmaids serve drinks in three circular bars, but the drinks are delivered to tables by (fully clothed) waiters.

There are, of course, just as many bars where a skilfully mixed cocktail can be sipped without distractions. The places that leap to mind are Hong Kong's world-class hotels. For a spectacular view, try the **Sky Lounge** in Tsimshatsui's Sheraton Hotel where the 18-floor ascent is via a glass elevator running up outside the building. Others in search of greenery will enjoy the atrium lounge of the **Royal Garden Hotel** while for close-up views of Hong Kong's busy harbour, what could be more magnificent than the sweep of the floor-to-ceiling window of the lobby bar of the **Regent Hotel**. Across the harbour, the **La Ronda** bar atop the Furama Hotel provides an equally fine view back to Kowloon, while those after a touch of graciousness need go no further than the **Captain's Bar** in the Mandarin Oriental or the vantage viewpoint of the elegant **Clipper Lounge** upstairs.

Moving downmarket, there are several pleasant bars imbued, to some degree, with a traditional British pub atmosphere. These do not feature bar girls. Instead, they have a different kind of feeling, decorated with wooden beams, dart boards, brass and leather, and serve hearty pub grub to go with the foaming tankards of draught British beer. The large **Bull and Bear**, on the ground floor of Hutchison House in Central, is always crowded, being one of the few pub-bars in that westerly part of the business centre in Hong Kong. Also popular are **The Jockey** in Swire House and **Mad Dogs** up on Wyndham Street. The **Old China Hand** at 104 Lockhart Road, Wanchai, is one of the smallest and cosiest; for something slick and noisy, try the **Dickens Bar** in the basement of the Excelsior Hotel in Causeway Bay — especially on Sundays for the live jazz or the regular Filipino pop combo.

On Kowloon side, the **White Stag**, 72 Canton Road, Tsimshatsui, with its copper-topped bar and wooden beams could be anybody's local country pub — even the menu is traditional. **The Blacksmith's Arms**, 16 Minden Avenue, Tsimshatsui, is more of an urban local and dishes up large servings of food. Most of these bars open around 11 am or noon and serve until 1 am or 2 am with a Happy Hour (cheaper prices) normally between 5 pm to 7 pm.

For music lovers, the **Godown** in the basement of Sutherland House, Chater Road, Central, has an unashamedly boisterous bistro atmosphere with live jazz and dancing. Another meeting place is **Hardy's Folk Club**, 35 D'Aguilar Street, Central, where guitarists of every style perform and guest artists are welcome. In the same area and just round the corner in Lan Kwai Fong is **Club 97** and **California**, both providing the latest in lively music and good food that typifies one aspect of the Hong Kong night scene.

Two other good places to hear music are the newly opened **The Wanch** on Lockhart Road, and **Joe Bananas**, 23 Luard Road, Wanchai, a trendy night spot which attracts an upmarket crowd to its atmosphere of art deco/pop-rock film posters and photography in which to enjoy live music and take advantage of a full menu.

On Kowloon side **Ned Kelly's Last Stand**, 11A Ashley Road, Tsimshatsui, has a rowdy Australian atmosphere of beer drinking without the frills, live jazz and a menu full of interesting-sounding Australian dishes. Another antipodean haven is the **Stoned Crow**, 12 Minden Avenue, Tsimshatsui, while **Rick's Cafe** at 4 Hart Avenue, Tsimshatsui, is known as a restaurant/bar/live-music/dance club that features some of the best sounds in town.

Disco fever has waned somewhat in Hong Kong since the heady days of *Saturday Night Fever* and many of the fast-buck versions have closed. **Disco Disco** is one of the longest running at 38 D'Aguilar Street, Central, and currently has a Ladies Night on Wednesdays. The atmosphere is lively and the music of a high standard. Also popular is the **Talk of the Town** in the Excelsior Hotel: newly refurbished in art deco pink and black, it enjoys a stunning view across the harbour (Ladies' Nights are Mondays and Wednesdays for which there is no cover charge). In a class by itself is **Canton**, Canton Road, Tsimshatsui, one of the smartest discos around with an atmosphere that seems to capture the spirit of Hong Kong exactly. Other popular nightspots can be found in the upmarket hotels around Tsimshatsui such as the New World Hotel's imaginatively decorated **Faces**, the electronic gadgetry of the **Falcon** in the Royal Garden Hotel or **Hollywood East** (basement, Hotel Regal Meridien) with its hi-tech lighting effects and ultra-modern decor.

The cheapest form of night entertainment traditionally presented to tourists is the night market. Best known is the so-called **Poor Man's Nightclub** on Hong Kong Island which is set up each evening on the west side of the Victoria Hotel building (Shun Tak Centre, next to the Macau Ferry Pier) and dismantled again around 11 pm. Despite its name, this nightclub is simply a lively market selling cheap clothes and tourist trinkets and where most locals head for the seafood in the market's stalls — clams, prawns, mussels, tiger snails. You make your choice and then watch as the food is plunged into bubbling cauldrons of water. The seafood is undoubtedly fresh and appetizing — the surroundings where you eat it less so. The Kowloon version takes place along **Temple Street** and is no less entertaining with its mixture of bric-a-brac vendors, fortune tellers and busy food stalls.

There are also a number of ways that Hong Kong's transport comes into its own to show another and more romantic side of the territory. These range from the various sunset and night tours organised by **Watertours** (tel. 5-254808, 5-263538), tram parties (tel. 5-8918765) as well as a ride on the Peak Tram to enjoy the million-dollar night view from the top of the Peak. For those of more artistic bent, a whole range of cultural events takes place after nightfall, including plays, recitals, concerts and showcase traditional Chinese performances, and for these, again, you should consult your visitor's newspaper or check with the HKTA whose leaflets will keep you fully informed.

Elaborately choreographed dancers in dazzling costumes usually belong to the hotspots of Macau, but one-off shows featuring well-known entertainers are staged several times a year in the **Pink Giraffe** in the Sheraton. The **Hilton** produces a 'dinner theatre' two or three times a year and flies in a cast from a popular West End production. Some of the enormous Chinese restaurants provide traditional Chinese floor shows with a meal, and these can be misleadingly advertised as nightclubs although they provide one of the easiest ways to come in contact with the Cantonese taste in entertainment.

A successful mingling of food with local colour can be experienced at the Aberdeen **floating restaurants**, although you should be prepared to be entertained by the general ambiance rather than any particularly memorable culinary experience.

Finally, mention must be made of the **Hong Kong Arts Centre**, 2 Harbour Road, Wanchai, and its regular programmes of music, films and plays including visiting artists, and the more bohemian **Fringe Club** at 2 Lower Albert Road, Hong Kong — all contributing to Hong Kong's kaleidoscope of night-time activity.

Museums

Hong Kong is uniquely placed to record and study Chinese history and culture. For the moment the territory has no single large museum, although ambitious plans are being made for the Cultural Complex, due to open next to the Kowloon Star Ferry terminus in 1989. The past 20 years have seen the opening of a number of small museums. Because their size is so limited, these are highly selective and are all very good.

Space Museum

Of the four centrally located museums, the Space Museum — on the Kowloon waterfront opposite the Peninsula Hotel — offers the most spectacular experience.

Opened in October 1980, this HK$60-million project consists of a 300-seat Space Theatre, a Hall of Solar Sciences, an Exhibition Hall, a lecture hall, astronomy bookshop and snack bar.

Whatever the **Space Theatre**'s programme (changed roughly every six months) you can be sure it will be both beautiful and dramatic. Films are projected onto the 75-foot diameter domed roof. In the centre of the auditorium a weird-looking space monster — in fact the Zeiss Planetarium projector — moves up and down on its axis throughout the hour-long show; in addition there is an Omnimax projector with over 100 precision lenses capable of slotting onto a gigantic 'fish eye', many special effects projectors, and a multi-channel sound system — all automatically controlled by a computer in the centre of the theatre. The result is both absorbing and spectacular. The entire screen is used throughout the show, which means you have an equally good vantage point no matter where you sit. All screenings have Cantonese commentary, but headphones at every seat provide English, Japanese or Mandarin versions.

The sun is of course the theme of the **Hall of Solar Sciences**. A solar telescope gives the visitor a close look at the anatomy of the star on which we all depend. Other exhibits delve into subjects such as solar phenomena and solar energy with copious use of audiovisual devices and microcomputers; and before you leave, a quizzing computer can test the knowledge acquired during your visit to the Hall. The **Exhibition Hall** deals with man's advancement in the fields of astronomy and space exploration. One of the most interesting exhibits is the Aurora 7 space capsule in which Scott Carpenter made three orbits of the earth in 1962. Telephone 3-7212361 for current programme times and other details. The exhibition halls are open from 2–10 pm Monday–Saturday, 10.30 am–10 pm Sunday and public holidays, and are closed on Tuesday. Tickets are available at the museum, for an all-in price of HK$15.

Museum of History

This is now in two pre-war buildings in Kowloon Park, a little way up Nathan Road, past the Hyatt Hotel. Exhibits chart Hong Kong's archaeological and ethnological background and development. A highlight of the permanent exhibition is a series of detailed models of fishing junks and their tackle, illustrating traditional fishing methods. Special exhibitions, such as 'Hong Kong Before 1841', are invariably fascinating, clearly captioned and well laid out. Those especially interested in 19th- and 20th-century Hong Kong should ask to see the museum's albums of old photographs, which provide a revealing insight into the Territory's development and social life. From time to time major exhibitions are brought in from outside Hong Kong: watch for announcements of these as they are always superb.

Hong Kong Museum of Art

On Hong Kong Island beside the Star Ferry is the Hong Kong Museum of Art on the 10th and 11th floors of the City Hall High Block. On the 10th floor you will find a selection from the museum's permanent collection of Chinese art and antiquities, while on the 11th floor you will find special exhibitions, covering a broad spectrum of contemporary and historic Chinese and Western art.

This museum is sadly hampered by its limited floor area, but careful selection and rotation of displays must suffice until the new Cultural Complex museums and galleries are ready. Over the past two decades a fine collection has been built up in anticipation of the move. Attractive and inexpensive postcards and prints, plus a number of interesting publications are on sale at the museum. Opening times are 10 am—6 pm on weekdays (closed Thursdays) and Sundays 1 pm—6 pm.

Fung Ping Shan Museum

Further afield at the University of Hong Kong in Pokfulam is the Fung Ping Shan Museum. This imposing building, with its circular main exhibition hall, was originally opened in 1953 primarily as a teaching museum for the university's art students. The bronze and early pottery collections are particularly fine. The earliest pieces are ritual vessels from the Shang (1600—1027 BC) to Zhou (1027—256 BC) Dynasties. There are bronze mirrors from the Han (206 BC—AD 220) to Tang

(618–907) Dynasties. Also notable is the collection of 967 Nestorian Crosses, dating back to the Yuan Dynasty (1279–1368). The Nestorian creed is thought to have reached China in the Tang Dynasty, well before Marco Polo's arrival. It managed to survive the intervening centuries to regain favour under Khublai Khan, who created a Nestorian archbishopric in Peking in 1275. The museum also houses a fine ceramic collection of late Ming and Ch'ing paintings. Opening times 9.30 am–6 pm daily. Closed on Sundays and public holidays.

Art Gallery

The Art Gallery at the Chinese University of Hong Kong at Ma Liu Shui, just north of Shatin, in the New Territories, is also predominantly for the purpose of teaching. Located in the middle of the university's impressive, modern campus, you enter the gallery via a contemporary interpretation of a traditional Chinese courtyard garden. Abundant decorative carp flourish in the miniature canals around the perimeter. The interior exhibition space is on four split levels. The museum houses several important collections, of which the most notable are the Jen Yu-wen collection, consisting of 1,300 items from the Ming Dynasty to recent times, and the Min Chui Society of Hong Kong's bequest of 463 exquisite Ming jade flowers. Opening times 9.30 am–4.30 pm daily, Sundays 12.30 pm–4.30 pm.

Lei Cheng Uk

The Lei Cheng Uk Branch Museum (part of the Museum of History) houses a well-preserved tomb of the Eastern Han Dynasty (25–220). Following the devastating squatter hut fires of 1954, the tomb was discovered during the foundation work for Hong Kong's first public housing estate at Shek Kip Mei. Subsequent excavation was carried out by the University of Hong Kong and the find was opened to the public in 1957. Driving through this densely populated concrete jungle one suddenly comes upon an incongruous grassy knoll beside a park. In front of the tomb stands a small museum building which exhibits drawings and stone rubbings depicting life in Han times, as well as actual rubbings from the tomb's patterned bricks and photographs recording the excavation of the site. Replicas of a person's worldly possessions to help in the after-life have always played a part in Chinese burial custom, and on display are numerous bronze and pottery items found in the tomb: charming model houses complete with animal yards, and pottery storage jars, much like those found today in many a rustic kitchen. Opening times 10 am–1 pm and 2 pm–6 pm daily (closed Thursdays) and Sundays 1 pm–6 pm.

The Museum of Chinese Historical Relics

Opened in 1984, this 13,000-square-foot museum is a permanent exhibition site for cultural treasures from China. The display changes twice a year and features some of China's most dramatic and beautiful recent archaeological discoveries. The museum is equipped with pre-recorded tapes in English or Cantonese and an expert is available to answer questions. Located in the Causeway Centre, near the Wanchai Ferry Pier, the museum is open from 10 am to 6 pm virtually every day of the year. Admission HK$20 (students and children HK$10), HK$5 for groups of 10 persons or more. For further information telephone 5-8320411.

Flagstaff House Museum of Tea Ware

The Flagstaff House Museum of Tea Ware is housed in the oldest Western-style building still standing in Hong Kong. Located in Victoria Barracks, just off Cotton Tree Drive, its elegant verandahs, tiled roof and tree-shaded setting charmingly conjure up the atmosphere of the mid-19th century when it was built. A number of other Victorian buildings in the barracks have been given a new lease of life, most notably the Marriage Registry to the right of the main entrance gate.

The collection includes about 500 pieces of tea ware mainly of Chinese origin dating from the Warring States Period up to the present day, among which Yixing teapots are the most notable. There is also a special display on the history of tea. Opening hours: 10 am–5 pm except Wednesday.

The Sam Tung Uk Museum

As the 'satellite' industrial town of Tsuen Wan grew up in the New Territories over the past decade, three lines of 200-year-old houses survived intact. These formed the clan home of the Chan family, immigrants from Fujian province. At the end of 1987, Sam Tung Uk became Hong Kong's newest museum, containing period house displays and giving a lively insight into the lifestyle of the scholar class during the Ch'ing Dynasty (1644–1911). Ironically, as part of the process of metamorphosis the original buildings were demolished and what you see today are reinforced cement replicas. Nevertheless the place is worth visiting and it is readily accessible, being only minutes away from the Tsuen Wan MTR station.

Historic Buildings

In the face of the myriad skyscrapers, it would be easy to think of Hong Kong as having no past. But in fact the place did not spring up fully armed like dragon's teeth, and many reminders of the past await the patient explorer in search of another time and place. As far back as prehistoric times the earliest inhabitants left huge rock carvings, pottery and gigantic log slides. Central itself has its share of historic buildings in among the high-tech sites. Most visible is the former Supreme Court building which now houses the Legislative Council Chambers. Completed in 1912, its massive lines look particularly graceful when illuminated at night.

Another former court building lies only 200 yards (182 metres) away, behind Beaconsfield House, on Battery Path. What was for long Victoria District Court, the former French Mission, has had a chequered history since it was first built in the mid-19th century. Restored in 1987 to an approximation of its 1915 lines, it now serves as an annex to the Government Information Service, and it also houses the Hong Kong office of the World Wildlife Fund. The outside is charming in a dignified, restrained way, and the elegant proportions of the interior chapel create one of the most beautiful rooms in Hong Kong.

Go east, past St John's Cathedral, under or over Garden Road and Cotton Tree Drive, to Victoria Barracks with its 19th-century buildings built for British army families. The marriage registry is housed in one of these buildings and bridal parties make a charming sight on sunny days. The treasure of the barracks is undoubtedly Flagstaff House. Completed in 1846, this is the oldest type of Colonial building still standing in Hong Kong. Now a museum of Chinese tea ware, it was the official residence of the Commander of the British Forces in Hong Kong until 1979 when the entire barracks passed to the Hong Kong Government.

For a feeling of what life must have been like a century ago, walk up into Central Police Station compound, which stands where Hollywood Road becomes Wyndham Street. The magistracy in the same complex dates from 1914, but most of the other buildings are known to be considerably older.

An equally interesting police station is the Marine Police Headquarters in Tsimshatsui, dating from 1884. With its deep verandahs, watch towers and Round House — in use until the 1930s for the midday time signal — this enclave of the past was originally on the waterfront. Reclamation has stranded it some distance from the sea, but it is still used by the Marine Police.

Because of heavy development on Hong Kong Island, you will find most of the more interesting old Chinese buildings in the New Territories. It can be difficult to date rural temples, houses and ancestral halls with any certainty as rebuilding on the same site was commonplace through the centuries. Thus a temple might be described as 800 years old, although it was perhaps totally rebuilt 250 years ago and at least partially changed in the last century.

If you find you have a taste for Chinese traditional architecture, look at a large scale map and try exploring places where you see a temple indicated. Villages with the word *wai* or *tsuen* included in their names are worth exploring. To help you in this, the Hong Kong Museum of History sells a book entitled *History Around Us*, which considerably amplifies the admittedly arbitrary selection that follows.

Many villages have changed little in several centuries, and most have some unusual features worth seeking out. Look at roof ridges, glance above doorways and peer under dark roofs to see the massive groups of interlocking beams which hold together many traditional buildings. Villagers will not exactly welcome you with open arms, but provided you observe the usual rules of courtesy and common sense, you will rarely encounter any hostility.

Railway buffs should not miss the chance to walk on the disused sleepers, clamber through old coaches and play with the signal levers at the **Tai Po Railway Museum**. When the railway line was fully electrified, the tiny station at Tai Po Market became obsolete. The

pretty Chinese decorations and roof trimmings have been repainted, shrubs have been planted around it and a modest collection of memorabilia from the beginning of the Kowloon-Canton Railway has been installed. Go out on the tracks to get a good look at the painted bats under the eaves.

Only two minutes away, after the street market selling everything from spinach to fluorescent pink socks, stands the **Man Mo Temple**. In 1986, this was in a terrible state, with the back wall in danger of collapsing. Now, HK$600,000 later, it has a new roof and substantial sections of new wall. The courtyard has been spruced up and the place provides a focus for the whole community.

New Territories clans are powerful and wealthy, as you will appreciate at the enormous **Man Lung Fung** ancestral hall at San Tin. This is virtually deserted except at festival time. Walk around the courtyards and admire the subtle lines of beams which rise instead of lying truly horizontal. The Mans came to this area from Kianghsi (Jiangxi) Province in the 15th century. The hall is believed to have been built about 300 years ago. To reach San Tin, turn off the Castle Peak Road where you see the signs for Wing Ping Tsuen and San Tin.

Not far away is one of the territory's most magnificent buildings, the **Tai Fu Tai**. Ask for directions to find it among the clusters of traditional village houses. Until recently the building was the preserve of squatters. It is currently undergoing substantial, and sensitive restoration, thanks to a HK$2.6 million grant from the Royal Hong Kong Jockey Club. In the 1860s this was the home of an important government official. It is richly adorned with carvings, mouldings and other embellishments of uniformly fine quality. The pottery decorations on the roof ridge are from the Shiwan Wen Ru-bi kiln, one of the most famous in southern China, and they date from 1865.

Festivals

All the world loves a festival, an excuse for colour, feasting and a change from routine. The Chinese are no exception to this rule, and Hong Kong's calendar is punctuated by festivals of many types. Some are major celebrations, marked by processions, operatic productions, firework displays and similar public happenings on a large scale. Others are equally significant, but take the form of intensely personal devotions, inaccessible to outsiders. Unless you are fortunate enough to have Chinese friends, you will have to be content with the public faces of local festivals.

Most Hong Kong people are only one or two generations removed from the soil. Their peasant ancestors followed the whims of the seasons, the phases of the moon and possible signs that this might be the right time to plough, to plant or to harvest. They needed the security of a vast almanac telling them what was appropriate on every day of the year. Life in today's highrises has changed beyond recognition in most respects, but the lunar calendar still dictates many of Hong Kong's public holidays in celebration of major Chinese festivals as well as such traditional Western holidays as Christmas and Easter.

Festivals are family-centred occasions. For centuries the two major events of the year — Chinese New Year (nowadays renamed the Spring Festival in the People's Republic of China) and the Mid-Autumn Festival — were the only times of reunion for far-flung relatives. Today most small- to medium-sized factories and workshops in Hong Kong still close down completely for as long as two weeks at this time of the year. The owners say they find it easier to give all employees their statutory 14 days of annual holiday at the same time, rather than stagger leave dates throughout the year. And certainly the employees seem to favour this approach, many seizing the chance to travel, visiting relatives in China, or venturing further afield.

The major festivals are all marked by a public holiday, although in recent years the tendency has been to observe it the day after to allow everyone to recover from late-night celebrations. Minor festivals take place virtually every day, although only a few members of the older generation follow them all faithfully, with the help of the almanac, still issued annually.

Some of the most interesting festivals are little known outside a particular section of the community — the boat people, or the residents of a single island or walled village in the New Territories, for instance. The HKTA can supply a list of events, which will include some of these, such as the Cheung Chau Bun Festival. Others like the

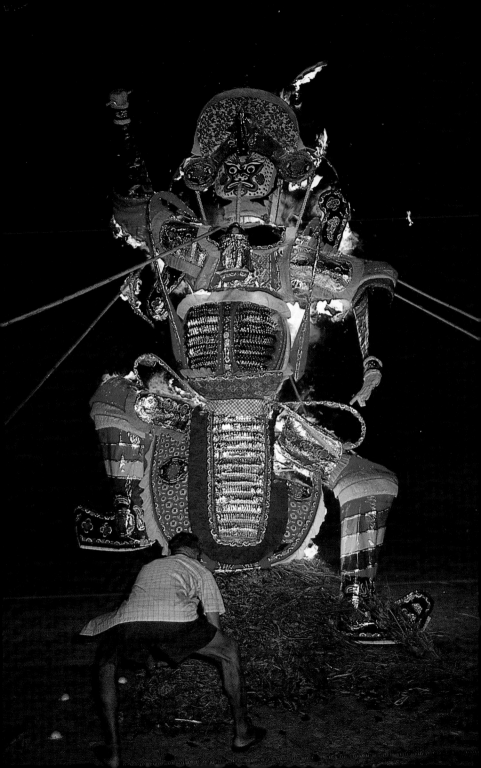

Ten-Year — or even more important 100-Year — clan celebrations may only be encountered by chance.

The easiest signs to spot as you tour the rural areas of Hong Kong are the temporary theatre and other structures put up for these celebrations, usually on open ground outside a village. Made of bamboo, with tin sheets for roofing, these are minor marvels of traditional engineering in themselves. The design has probably varied little in the past 1,000 years, although these days for the most part they are held together with plastic stays rather than the traditional rattan bindings. The biggest of these 'matsheds', as they are known, is the theatre for performances of Chinese opera to entertain the gods, whose colossal paper effigies are housed in their own matshed. A smaller structure houses a communal kitchen.

Outsiders will attract plenty of stares, but are always tolerated at such events, if they take the time to walk around. Even in the daytime there is a bustling, festive atmosphere. Visitors light joss sticks, chat and bargain for windmills, gilt bells and other souvenirs. If the community is rich, opera may continue round the clock, by relays of performers, the best being reserved for the show late in the evening. Do not be surprised to find yourself virtually the only person in the audience in the daytime.

With the exception of a few fanatics, the Chinese attitude to religion has never been dogmatic. The sixth-century scholar Fu Hsi was the epitome of Chinese eclecticism; he dressed in a Taoist cap, a Buddhist scarf and Confucian shoes. In more recent centuries, Western missionaries were appalled when converts simply absorbed the trinity into their existing collection of deities. The popular belief has always been that it is impossible to have too many gods: each represents additional insurance — for this world or the next.

The official figures list a total of 600 temples in the whole of Hong Kong, of which 100 represent a mixture of religions, while 300 are Buddhist and 200 are Taoist. Temples go in and out of fashion. If a devotee obtains valuable advice when consulting the wooden fortune sticks or other sources of guidance, word spreads fast and the temple is soon buzzing with worshippers in search of similar good luck. This may continue for months or years, the profits from sales of *heung yau* (incense and lamp oil) plus donations from the faithful going into extensive and often bizarre renovations or innovations. Such popularity is as fickle as fate, waning as readily as it waxes, leaving some of Hong Kong's most interesting temples virtually deserted year round.

The **Lunar New Year** — or Chinese New Year — which falls in late January or early February is the most widely observed festival. Each year is assigned to one of 12 animals (which follow each other in rotation), each possessing different characteristics: the legend concerning this 12-year cycle tells how the Lord Buddha summoned to him all earth's animals but only 12 obeyed and, as a reward for their loyalty, he named a year after each one. Your fate in any one year may be determined by the relationship between the animal of the year in question and that of the year of your birth. The coming of a New Year means a period of goodwill, the settling of debts and quarrels and a visit to the fortune-teller. Ancestors are worshipped — the spirit of an uncared-for ancestor can turn very nasty — and special attention is paid to the Kitchen God, for it is thought that at the end of each year he returns to the Jade Emperor to report on the family's conduct during the past year. Special food is prepared, often vegetarian, and presents of New Year biscuits (*chau mai beng*, stamped with messages such as 'Harmony and Prosperity', 'May sons and wealth be yours') are exchanged. To the delight of children they are given little red *lai si* packets containing money — the colour red being lucky. Everywhere you will hear or see the words *Kung Hei Fat Choi* (Best wishes and prosperity) though to young couples the greeting is *Kung Hei Tïm Ding* (Best wishes and have more sons).

However, for the visitor this thoroughly family festival can be a bleak time. The statutory holiday spans three days but many shops and restaurants close for two weeks. Hundreds of thousands of people return to China to visit relatives — so it is definitely not the best time for a quick trip across the border. Central District, though dressed in decorative lights with the animal of the year shining down from prominent buildings, tends to be deserted. To get an authentic feeling of this festival, visit one of the special new year fairs in the final week of the old year. Fragrant Chinese narcissi, huge blossom-covered peach branches and mini orange trees are given as symbols of long life and prosperity. The oranges are later dried and stewed to make medicine. The largest market is in Victoria Park, Causeway Bay, where, especially at night, there are row upon row of exquisite blooms, food stalls, side shows and thousands of jostling men, women and children in holiday mood. The end of Chinese New Year, on the 15th day, is marked by the lighting of traditional lanterns.

The **Springtime Birthday of Tin Hau**, the (Taoist) Empress of Heaven, is lavishly celebrated. She is the patron saint of fishermen and they depend on her to keep them safe throughout the year. Many temples in her honour can be found in the territory, although thanks to reclamation, many are now well back from their original waterfront vantage point. The most popular temple is in Joss House Bay and dates from 1266. The harbour becomes a sea of rippling silken banners as convoys of boats sail to this remote rendezvous.

Roast suckling pigs, joss sticks and other offerings are made ashore, where the insistent drumming of lion dance teams heightens the festive atmosphere. Individual boat shrines are taken into the temple to be blessed for another year by the Taoist priest. It is estimated that 20,000 people visit this tiny temple during the birthday celebrations. So be prepared for dense crowds if you decide to go along. Special commercial tours are organised for the festival and there are usually excursion ferries too.

Many legends surround Tin Hau's earthly existence. The daughter of a 10th-century Fukien (Fujian) fisherman, she is reputed to have sailed on a straw mat into the eye of a typhoon and guided an entire fishing fleet to safety. Faith in her supernatural powers continued to grow after her death until, in the Ch'ing Dynasty (1644–1911), she was given the title Empress of Heaven.

In May the three-day **Cheung Chau Bun Festival** is celebrated. Three vast wooden towers, each covered with some 5,000 white buns, stamped with a goodwill message, are erected near Pak Tai Temple. The purpose of these bun towers is to appease the hungry spirits of pirate victims, whose mutilated bodies were found in the 1880s on this small, dumbbell-shaped island on the west side of Hong Kong's archipelago. This Taoist festival also gives thanks to Pak Tai, Emperor of the North and God of the Sea, for protecting the islanders since the 1770s from various plagues. The festivities include Chinese opera, lion dances, stilt dances and a fabulous procession, featuring many legendary figures as well as more contemporary celebrities. Small children in elaborate costumes seem to float in mid-air. Get to the island early in the day and wander through the back streets to discover the secret of this particular brand of magic. At midnight on the third day a gong sounds and the destruction of the 60-foot bun towers begins. In the past young men scaled them with the object of collecting as many buns as possible — the higher the bun the greater the luck it was supposed to bring them. Since a tower accidentally collapsed, the scramble has been discontinued and the buns are distributed by the priests. Special tours go to the island for the festivities and there are also supplementary ferry sailings throughout this period.

The **Dragon Boat Festival** (*Tuen Ng*) in June is equally decorative and rather more accessible as the races are held in many parts of the territory. The races commemorate Chu Yuan, a fourth-century scholar, who was so distressed by the corruption of local government officials that he threw himself into the Mei Lo River in Hunan. To keep the fish from eating his corpse the local people scattered the water with rice dumplings and beat drums — perhaps as one sees Chinese fishermen today, rowing from one end of their net to another, beating a drum, or thrashing the water with a long stick, to scare the fish into their nets. Today the craft used for the races which celebrate

this distant event are long, slim and gaily painted, with the ornately carved head and tail of the fearsome dragon. Depending on their size, they carry ten or 20 oarsmen with an additional person acting as coxswain, beating on a large drum to keep time for the rowers. An international dragon boat competition is staged in the weeks following the festival and it usually draws teams from many parts of the world. The accompanying razzmatazz makes this, too, a colourful and enjoyable event.

Altogether more tranquil is the **Mid-Autumn Festival**. Traditionally this was a harvest festival, but it also had a political significance. During an uprising against the ruling Mongol Yuan Dynasty in the 14th century, messages were passed to conspirators in *moon cakes*. Today these cakes no longer contain messages, although they do have an exotic range of sweet and savoury fillings. The mixture includes pork fat, duck egg, lotus seeds, sugar and red bean — an acquired taste for most people. In the weeks before the festival sales are brisk and streets and markets are festooned with colourful lanterns. Some are in traditional shapes, like rabbits, starfruit and goldfish, while others are modern novelties like rockets and aeroplanes. On the night of the festival many families take their moon cakes and lanterns to one of the territory's peaks where they can enjoy the rising of the moon — always unusually large and brilliant at this season. In recent years a lantern carnival has been organised in Victoria Park, Causeway Bay, and another in the Ko Shan Theatre in Kowloon. These feature displays of magnificent lanterns as well as opera and other entertainment. The sight of the lanterns flickering among the trees is one of the prettiest experiences Hong Kong has to offer. Make the effort to visit the Peak or one of the parks.

Ching Ming in the spring and **Chung Yeung** in the autumn are the times when families visit the graves of their ancestors, to clean them and make offerings. There's nothing morbid about the rituals which are usually rather colourful, informal family picnics.

Yue Lan is the Festival of Hungry Ghosts, who are released from the underworld for one lunar month. At this time food and paper offerings are prepared to appease the spirits of the dead. At the side of the road, particularly in residential areas, you may see some elaborate paper models of houses, motor cars, horses and furniture waiting to be burned to help the spirits on their way.

The **Winter Solstice** in the third week of December is the third most important festival in the Chinese calendar and it catches most non-Chinese completely by surprise. There is no public holiday, and the celebration is very much a family affair. Most smaller shops and offices close early or take the whole day off, and many taxi drivers take at least half a day off, too.

Sport

Given the shortage of land in Hong Kong its citizens are surprisingly well provided with sporting facilities. Practically every sport from wheelchair archery to softball is catered to, although given Hong Kong's climate and coastline the emphasis naturally tends to be on water-related activities. The opening of the Queen Elizabeth Stadium in Happy Valley, the Victoria Park exhibition tennis courts, and the Hong Kong Coliseum (this HK$115 million project built over the railway terminus seats 12,500 spectators under cover) have all made it possible for Hong Kong to stage international sporting events.

Beyond any doubt, the most popular sport of all in Hong Kong is horse-racing. This is explained more by the Chinese love of gambling rather than a love of the horses themselves. Although the Royal Hong Kong Jockey Club was founded in 1884, professional racing was only introduced in the mid-1970s. In the 1984−85 season the total amount wagered was US$2.5 billion, which equates to an average per race of an incredible US$3.7 million. The Jockey Club administers Hong Kong's racing and holds the government betting monopoly (Hong Kong's only legal form of gambling unless one counts the stock market).

Racecourses are at Happy Valley and Shatin. The latter was completed in 1978 and is equipped with every conceivable modern luxury including piped music in the stables and heated swimming pools for the horses. The centre of the course is a beautifully landscaped park, open to the public on non-race days. The stands are packed, with attendance per meeting averaging 34,600 people. Race-goers sit poring over their newspapers, or listening to the latest totalizer odds on their transistors. Shatin has the world's biggest trackside video matrix·on which punters in the stands can read the rapidly changing odds, or watch a close-up of the action. It also provides slow motion film and instant replay of a race, and displays information in English and Chinese (the messages being illustrated by animated cartoons). Few race-goers ever venture down to see the actual horses in the paddock. Because of the money involved the air crackles with tension at the start of each race, building up to a crescendo roar from the anxious crowd at the finish.

The racing season runs from September to May and if you would like to go to the races in style, the HKTA organises *Come Horse Racing* tours. You must be a bona fide visitor in Hong Kong for less than 21 days to participate.

Every year the Jockey Club donates a sizeable proportion of its huge surplus to charity and other sports-related facilities such as the Queen Elizabeth Stadium and the Jubilee Sports Centre alongside the

Shatin racetrack. The latter is a HK$150 million project which
provides everything a budding athlete could desire: it is designed to
coach Hong Kong's international athletes of the future.

Health conscious visitors are able to jog along the Jubilee Sports
Centre's 'trim trail' from 7 am to 7 pm. A number of Hong Kong's
urban and country parks and public housing estates have similar trails.
Ask your hotel where to find the nearest one. There are also several
gyms (including Tom Turk's Fitness Club and Clark Hatch Physical
Fitness Centre, Nautilus Health Centre) and dance and exercise classes
(Arts Centre) readily available in Central District and Kowloon. The
YMCA organises classes in yoga, judo, *tai chi ch'uan* and martial arts.
For visiting golfers, the Royal Hong Kong Golf Club has three 18-hole
courses at Fanling in the New Territories and nine holes at Deepwater
Bay (on Hong Kong Island) but they are available to non-members on
weekdays only. The Clearwater Bay Golf and Country Club (in
Saikung, tour by HKTA on weekdays) and the Discovery Bay Golf
Club (on Lantau Island 8 am—8 pm daily) each have an 18-hole
course, plus other recreational facilities such as tennis courts and
swimming pool. Tennis enthusiasts can use any of the public courts,
although booking can be difficult. You can only book a day in advance
(by going in person, with your passport). These courts have no
equipment for hire, but the Excelsior Hotel Sports Deck — with both
tennis courts and golf range — does.

For water sports such as water skiing and wind surfing, ring the
HKTA, which will provide names and numbers to contact. For
underwater sports contact either the Hong Kong Underwater
Federation or the YMCA Scuba Club.

Country Parks/Open Spaces

Walking boots might not be the first item you would pack for a trip to
Hong Kong, but if you enjoy wide open spaces, the solitude of
mountain tops and the call of woodland birds, you may well find
yourself making a quick visit to one of Hong Kong's many shoe shops
to buy some sneakers before setting off to explore the less well-known
side of the territory.

Hong Kong's buildings are packed so densely together that it can
come as a surprise to realise about three-quarters of the total land area
is without buildings of any sort. No matter where you stand in the city,
it is almost always possible to see hills, luring you to explore.

Despite Hong Kong's perennial land-development hunger, where it
seems every square centimetre must yield a quick profit, around 40
percent of the total area of 1,070 square kilometres (413 square miles)
is officially designated as country parks, which means there can never
be any building. The 21 parks plus two 'Special Areas', as they are
described, cover many types of landscape — including some of Hong
Kong's most beautiful beaches and rocky shores, as well as soaring
mountain chains rising to almost 1,000 metres (3,300 feet).

The parks range from the 4,477 hectares (11,062 acres) of Saikung
East, to the 270-hectare (667-acre) reservoir catchment area that is
diminutive Pokfulam Park. The terrain varies from the bleak grandeur
of the Pat Sin Range and much of Lantau, to fine, golden sand off
Saikung Peninsula and thickly-forested Tai Lam and Tai Po Kau.

Hong Kong's actual open land area may be limited compared to
that of other places, but it encompasses an amazing diversity of
features. Despite many common boundaries, each country park is
unique in some respect. Whether you fancy a gentle stroll along
shaded paths or a strenuous climb rewarded by a 360-degree
panoramic view, the parks offer you an experience of Hong Kong far
removed from the glitzy shopper's paradise that is the everyday tourist
beat.

You may see traditional Chinese omega-shaped graves on slopes
overlooking the sea. These are always sited with great attention paid to
the principles of *fung shui* (literally wind and water). The science is
often translated as geomancy, and experts dictate everything from
where you place your goldfish tank and office desk, to which building
you should live in and when you should marry. In most parts of Hong
Kong you can see eight-sided mirrors which is believed to deflect bad
fortune. As you pass traditional settlements, look out for *fung shui*
woods. These were planted near villages, newly-established as far back
as three or more centuries ago. Different varieties of bamboo plus

many trees with medicinal powers have been allowed to flourish in magnificent profusion. Once your eyes tune in you can soon pick out other features which are clearly part of the *fung shui* system.

The MacLehose Trail in the New Territories, is named after one of Hong Kong's former governors who was very active in promoting the Country Parks concept in Hong Kong. Linking eight parks, it stretches for 100 kilometres (62 miles), through some of Hong Kong's most beautiful and remote areas, including the territory's highest mountain — Tai Mo Shan.

Detailed leaflets highlighting the features of individual parks and the MacLehose Trail are available from the Agriculture and Fisheries Department headquarters, 393 Canton Road, Kowloon. As you go into each park you will find an information centre and detailed map of its special attractions.

Thanks to its geographical position — just within the tropics — Hong Kong's plant and bird life is unusually rich. And virtually all the 2,500 species of flowering and green plants, trees and ferns can be found within the country parks. Azaleas light up low ground and hillsides in late spring, while tiny blue gentians carpet mountain tops in early summer. Orchids and ferns lurk in unexpected places at all seasons, a surprise to the innocent eye. Hong Kong's native plants are protected by law, which should encourage them to flourish more abundantly with every passing season.

Such rich plant life in turn encourages abundant butterflies, some of which are relatively rare in world terms. Local moths include the giant silk worm moths, of which the Atlas has an average wing span of 23 centimetres and the Moon, 18 centimetres (7.09 inches). More than 200 recorded species and forms of butterflies have been found here. Between April–May and September–November, almost overwhelming numbers of these gaudy, fragile creatures may be encountered at any turn of the path as you explore.

Hong Kong's indigenous animal life has been much reduced by urbanisation and most of the remaining species (barking deer, pangolin, porcupine and wild pig among them) are nocturnal anyway, so your chances of seeing them are slim. Birds, however, are more resilient in the face of progress and you do not need to be a keen ornithologist to enjoy their presence.

Serious birdwatchers have a number of favourite spots. Some excellent books are available on Hong Kong birds, the best of which is undoubtedly the recently revised *New Colour Guide to Hong Kong Birds*, by Clive Viney and Karen Phillipps, published by the Government Printer, Hong Kong. The Hong Kong Bird Watching Society arranges regular field trips for its members, and if you would like to participate during your stay, contact the HKTA which will put you in touch with the appropriate person.

The Mai Po Nature Reserve (see page 150) is a collection of mudflats, fishponds and mangrove swamps in the extreme northwest of the New Territories, partly inside the closed border area with China. It constitutes a unique environment for migrant and resident birds. More than 250 species of birds have been recorded in this area, at least 110 of them rarely encountered elsewhere in the territory. On account of its international significance, the Reserve is administered by the World Wildlife Fund (WWF). Access is freely available to the WWF information centre at Mai Po, but the bird watching hides lie within the closed border area, which can only be entered with a permit. WWF organises guided tours every Wednesday, Thursday, Saturday, Sunday and Public Holidays; the price is HK$30 per head. Tickets should be collected in advance from WWF's head office in Central. Telephone 5-261011 for further information.

During the breeding season from April to July at the Yim Tso Ha Egretry near Shataukok, you can see as many as 1,000 egrets, including a few pairs of the very rare Swinhoe's Egret, plus as many as six species of herons. You cannot enter the egretry, but with the help of binoculars you can have an excellent view from the perimeter.

Public transport takes you to your starting point when exploring Hong Kong's open spaces. Most weekdays you can be sure to have the destination of your choice more or less to yourself — unless you have chosen the same day and the same place as a swarm of schoolchildren out for a picnic or field trip. Keep walking — few of them will venture far from their jumping off point. The same applies to weekend and holiday excursions: use your initiative and it is easy to move beyond the hordes.

Remember also that Hong Kong's open spaces are by no means confined to country parks. A number of the Outlying Islands have not been included in the scheme, but they, too, make fascinating destinations (see page 154).

The Vegetation of Hong Kong

by Professor D.A. Griffiths
— *Department of Botany, University of Hong Kong*

Hong Kong lies just within the tropics, and therefore the climax or naturally evolved vegetation should be semi-deciduous or monsoon forest. However, man's influence in Hong Kong has been so great over such a long period of time that it is difficult to find anywhere here remnants of the original forest. Instead, the vegetation is now made up of many different plant communities which fall into three basic categories.

Natural Forest Very little original forest remains in Hong Kong, but it would undoubtedly have supported trees characteristic of cooler climates such as *Quercus, Castanopsis* and *Lithocarpus*, today seen in Tai Po Kau Nature Reserve. However, repeated activity by man destroyed these forests some two thousand years ago. In an attempt to re-establish the forest, the British administration in 1880 encouraged villagers to plant species of Pine: during the period 1867 to 1882, approximately 25 million Pine trees were planted on the coastal region of Hong Kong. Following the massive destruction of the forest during the war years 1940−45, a re-aforestation programme was initiated in which a wide variety of trees were planted. These areas of 'natural' forest can now be seen at Tai Po Kau, Shing Mun and Tai Lam Chung, the most common species of trees being *Castanopsis fissa, Quercus bambusaefolia, Cinnamomum camphora, Ficus fistulosa, Sterculia lanceolata, Schima superba* and *Celtis sinensis*. In addition to the trees, woody climbers such as *Dalbergia* and *Uvaria* form dense thickets, and shade-tolerant shrubs such as *Psychotria rubra, Chloranthus glaber* and *Ilex pubescens* form an understorey.

Many villages in the New Teritories were established early in the last century, and trees such as *Aquilaria sinensis* — the Joss stick tree — together with bamboo and *Ficus microcarpa* were planted around them. These *Fung Shui* groves represent some of the earliest plantings in Hong Kong and are found in small pockets in the New Territories.

Introduced species In addition to the forest trees, many exotic trees have been introduced into Hong Kong since late in the last century. These include *Tristanea conferta* — the Brisbane Box — which is a broad-leave fire-resistant, fast-growing tree; *Liquidamber formosana* — a tall and elegant tree producing attractive autumnal colours — and *Melaleuca leucodendron*, which are widely planted on the roadside throughout the New Territories. New species are continually being introduced into the tree flora of Hong Kong.

Shrubland Much of Hong Kong is covered by shrubland; the three most common species are *Rhodomyrtus tomentosa, Raphiolepis indica* and *Gordonia axillaris*, which are aggressive growers and form dense thickets on the hillsides. Smaller plant species such as *Baeckia frutescens* grow in more open areas, and some trees from the forest such as

Schefflera octophylla also grow as dwarf forms. The most common climbers in the scrub vegetation are *Smilax* and *Millettia*, and on the edges, often near roads, *Melastoma candidum* and *Lantana camara* produce attractive coloured flowers.

Grassland Two forms of grassland can be distinguished in Hong Kong. There is hill grassland on mountain areas above 300 metres where the most common grasses are *Ischaemum* and *Aruninella*. Also evident is old field grassland, developed on paddy and other formerly-irrigated soil in the New Territories. The most common species in this second type are *Alopecurus aequalis*, *Paspalum distichum*, *Panicum repens* and *Sacciolepis indica*. Following the burning of vegetation on the hillsides, whether accidental or deliberate, one of the first that appears is *Paspalum purpureum*, a giant grass referred to as Napier grass or Elephant grass. This is a highly aggressive colonizer and forms dense thickets in which the average height is in excess of two metres. Other giant grasses such as *Themeda triandra*, *Neyraudia reyaudiana* and *Miscanthus* occur on the edges of these grass areas. These grasses produce huge punicles of flowers which are extremely attractive and much sought after for flower arrangements.

Rare plants In addition to listing the more common endangered species, Hong Kong has recently listed a number of plants that are very rare species and which are likely to disappear from our environment unless protective, conservative measures are taken. Such plants include *Enkianthus quinqueflorus* and particularly *Camellia granthamiana*, which was restricted to one single bush on the slope of Tai Mo Shan when it was discovered in 1952. Other rare plants include species of *Magnolia*, *Rhododendron* and *Tutcheria spectabilis*, and recent conservation work at the University of Hong Kong has shown that the orchids *Anoectochilus yungianus* and *Pecteilis susannae* are extremely rare and, before 1970 when it was re-established, the former had been lost to science for over 40 years. The Hong Kong slipper orchid (*Paphiopedilum purpuratum*) is the most highly prized of our local orchids and is found in the New Territories in a very few areas.

Parks and Gardens Hong Kong has a Zoological and Botanical Garden which was established in 1864 and contains, in addition to common local plants, a wide selection of economically important plants from mainland China. Since 1878, the staff of the botanical gardens have worked in conjunction with the Hong Kong Government Herbarium staff on the collection, classification and economical importance of plants of Southern China, but during the war, and following the Japanese invasion, the garden itself was damaged. The herbarium, however, was preserved intact by being sent to Singapore, and it was returned to Hong Kong in 1948.

Readers who want more information on active research can call the Government Information Service at 5-8428777, and the Government Publications Centre on 5-235377 regarding the large collection of literature available.

Beaches

Hong Kong's rocky coastline is dotted with beaches. Some 38 of these, on the mainland and some islands, are maintained for public use — they are manned during the summer season by lifeguards and beach cleaners, and offer changing rooms, tents, barbecue pits, refreshments stalls and bathing rafts. The HKTA has a useful leaflet which shows all maintained beaches, lists the facilities and describes how to get there.

But however enthusiastic the HKTA may be, no realist would deny that the Territory's crowded beaches come a poor second to the glorious stretches of sand in nearby Malaysia, Thailand and the Philippines. There may be days when beach conditions in Hong Kong are near perfect. The sand at times may be clean, the water may be as clear as the South China Sea ever is, and midweek the beach may be almost deserted. But the chances of this magic combination are small. Winds and tides carry piles of debris (driftwood, plastic bags and far worse) onto all beaches at some time or other. Heavy rain leaves both sand and sea muddy and grey. On Saturday afternoons, Sundays and public holidays, huge crowds of garrulous swimmers with barbecues and radios descend on beaches almost everywhere in the Territory.

The best beaches in Hong Kong are inevitably the most inaccessible. If you have the time (and good weather) to devote a whole day to the beach, then it is possible to treat yourself to an interesting expedition that will give a glimpse of some of the most beautiful parts of Hong Kong. On Lantau the near 914-metre (3,000-foot) high Lantau and Sunset Peaks form a stunning backdrop to a string of long sandy beaches along the island's southern shores. On the mainland the beaches of Clearwater Bay in the Saikung Peninsula are mostly unspoilt and sometimes breathtakingly beautiful. The inaccessibility rule even applies to Hong Kong Island, where the least crowded beach is at Big Wave Bay.

Activities for Family Holidays

If you are in an unfamiliar city with young children it can be hard to find activities for them to enjoy. Hong Kong has its limitations and strengths in this respect. According to the age of your children, consider the following suggestions, many of which are referred to elsewhere in the text. Museums are not included in this list, as they have their own section, starting on page 72.

Hong Kong Parks, even the smallest ones, are well provided with clean sandpits for toddlers, roundabouts, swings and climbing frames, plus a variety of tricycle, bicycle, skateboard, and rollerskating rinks.

If you are staying in Central, try Brewin Path Playground, just to the left beyond the roundabout at the top of Garden Road, a stiff walk, but an easy HK$6 or so taxi fare; in Tsimshatsui, try Kowloon Park between Nathan Road and Austin Road. Enquire at your hotel or the HKTA for the nearest facilities in your area.

Swimming is a great way to cool down in the hot weather. Ask for a list of beaches, but avoid weekends and public holidays if you don't like crowds. If you don't like salt water and your hotel has no pool, try one of the public pools run by the Urban Council. They are well supervised and clean. Facilities at new ones like Aberdeen are excellent, including a toddlers' pool, several shallow teaching pools and a diving pool.

More expensive, but great for a family outing, is **Water World**, the aquatic fun park run by **Ocean Park**. Ocean Park itself also makes a good full day out. You don't need to take a tour, but can buy tickets (adults: HK$100, children: HK$50) including round-trip bus transport from MTR stations in Central, Admiralty and Tsimshatsui. Cine 2000, Atoll Reef, Wave Cove and Ocean Theatre are all feasible in wet weather, although you will get better value from your entrance ticket if you can enjoy fully the escalators, cable cars, aviary and myriad other outdoor attractions. Check scheduled feeding times for birds and marine creatures.

Most young children enjoy animals. If pigs, chickens and ducks in a magnificent landscaped setting sound appealing, arrange to take a picnic to the **Kadoorie Farm**. Telephone 0-981317 for details. There is no entrance charge, but you will need a car unless you are prepared for a considerable walk.

For a good half-day's excursion, take a ferry to Peng Chau where you can catch a *gai do* (or small motor boat) to the pier below the **Trappist Dairy**. Walk up to the dairy, pause to admire the contented-looking black-and-white cows and buy samples of their milk. Then walk on over the pass and down to Silvermine Bay where you can catch a ferry back to Hong Kong. This excursion is suitable for children 4–5 years and up.

Less strenuous, but fun for everyone, is a trip to the **Zoological and Botanical Gardens** just above Central. Go in the early morning and watch the mostly elderly exponents of *tai chi ch'uan* (Chinese Shadow Boxing), that incredibly graceful system of body training. Go in the late afternoon and catch the birds at their most voluble. However, if you want to be there at feeding time, you will have to arrive before 8 am.

Climb in and out of the coaches and operate the signals at the **Tai Po Railway Museum**, at Tai Po Market in the New Territories.

Find a giant coin-operated telescope and see how many buildings you can identify — try at Edinburgh Place (between Star Ferry and the City Hall) or Tsimshatsui next to the Star Ferry terminal.

Ride the Peak Tram to the terminus, then walk around **The Peak** or climb as close as possible to the summit (sunny weather only). Try the telescope here.

Board a Hong Kong tram for the ride of your life, along the northern shore of Hong Kong Island. Sit upstairs and trundle along the rails from one terminus to the other. Dismount any time you see something that warrants closer investigation.

The following activities are particularly suitable for wet weather:

Clothes-conscious teenagers will enjoy rummaging for bargains in the many factory outlets of World Wide House in Central, Granville Road in Tsimshatsui, Spring Garden Lane in Wanchai, and Stanley Market, etc. Serious shoppers should do their homework with the regularly-updated *Guide to Hong Kong Factory Bargains* by Dana Goetz.

Ride the high-tech escalators of the Hongkong and Shanghai Bank headquarters, located at No. 1 Queen's Road Central.

Go ice skating in Lai Chi Kok, or at Cityplaza, Taikoo Shing. Cityplaza 1 and 2 offer an immense variety of shops and restaurants under one roof.

Visit a Japanese department store and try the different types of food on sale. Daimaru in Causeway Bay reputedly has the best selection in its basement Food Hall.

Go to a really big *dim sum* restaurant — like the one in the City Hall in Central or the Ocean Terminal in Tsimshatsui, or even the Jumbo at Aberdeen — before midday and try every type of delicacy.

Go roller skating at Roller World, Cityplaza, or at Telford Gardens Sportsworld. If it is not raining and you have your own skates, try the free rinks in places like Victoria Park.

Look at the ghoulish cement frescoes and dioramas at the Tiger Balm Gardens (Aw Boon Haw Gardens) above Causeway Bay to see how many kinds of hell there are. The jade collection here is due to re-open to the public in May 1988.

Go to Ten-Pin Bowling at Brunswick Bowling Alley in Middle Road, Tsimshatsui (telephone 3-7393687) or at Mei Foo Sun Chuen (telephone 3-7425911).

Watch traditional craftsmen working with paper, flour paste, wire and other materials at the Excelsior Hotel Arcade in Causeway Bay, or in the Basement of the Empire Centre, Tsimshatsui East.

Visit the Sung Dynasty Village (including waxworks exhibition) and be transported back into the past. It is mostly under cover, making it feasible for wet weather, but more fun in sunshine.

Hong Kong Present and Future

by David Bonavia
— author of *The Chinese, Hong Kong 1997*

Whatever happens to Hong Kong after the transfer of sovereignty to the People's Republic of China in 1997, the place itself will still be here. There will be no point in doing away with the towering apartment and office blocks, the complex modern road system, as these make up much of the territory's earning-power today. Peking will not want to do away either with any of those factors which make the territory tick, though some of their actual uses of the place may be altered. A Government building may acquire a new function, a monument or some street names may be changed.

The better-known restaurants and hotels will continue functioning, if only to boost the already booming travel industry. By then China will have many modern hotels built by joint venture and so those in Hong Kong will be no exception. Although the quaint old trams will probably be gone by 1997, there will be no reason for China to tamper with the now 100-year-old Peak Tram funicular nor with the gleaming lines of the ever-expanding Mass Transit System (Underground Railway). The Outlying Islands and more remote parts of the New Territories will still provide trekking courses and camp-sites for the adventurous. Tourists will continue to find Hong Kong stimulating because of its residual colonial atmosphere. Others will be excited by the shopping and continue to relish the Oriental and Western food available.

Indeed the physical changes in Hong Kong over the past 20 years may be considerably greater than any which will take place under China's broad supervision in the 50 years from 1997 on, during which, according to agreement, it is to be permitted to retain its free economic and financial status.

How Hong Kong will affect China may be even more startling: the likelihood is that Hong Kong will influence surrounding areas of China and more distant parts with the message that capitalism works. Many of China's cities will by then be groping towards some of the ideas and principles that make Hong Kong work; already many attempts are being made on the Mainland to copy Hong Kong's success, though political and ideological considerations still stand in the way.

In the new climate, Hong Kong will need to guard against bureaucracy and graft, both of which loom menacingly over the socialist experience in China. Hong Kong has gone a long way towards reducing its own problems of this kind, but it could still slip back.

From an administrative viewpoint China will be taking over a smoothly functioning social unit of 5 to 6 million people when Hong Kong becomes a Special Administrative Region of the People's Republic of China in 1997. Medicine, taxation, public transport are all fairly well organised although the pressure on them is very great. The Chinese government has expressed hope that most of the Royal Hong Kong Police stay behind as a nucleus of a locally appointed force. Everywhere Peking will be looking for people experienced in the ways of Hong Kong to encourage continuity and prevent disruption in 1997. The transition will be aided by the fact that the Chinese people of Hong Kong have lived almost without a political system since 1841. Like Chinese everywhere, those in Hong Kong tend to occupy themselves with commerce and traditional trades, leaving the wider issues to those at the top, whether Chinese or foreign. This relative indifference towards politics as we know it has made it easier for Britain and China to work out a new political framework for Hong Kong, as there are few activists opposing the quasi-democratic system that is proposed. Those who feel uneasy about living in an appendage of a socialist system may leave to make a new life elsewhere if they have sufficient money or job skills.

Attractive though Hong Kong's touristic delights are for Westerners, it is important to realise that life for most people is a hectic struggle to make ends meet and build a properous middle-class society. European residents are mostly shielded from the rough realities of life in Hong Kong, as they generally command higher salaries and often more favourable terms of service than local people do. Nonetheless, the standard of living in Hong Kong is startlingly higher than in China, and when 1997 comes along there will doubtless be an increase in the pressure to enter Hong Kong, whether legally or illegally, and enjoy its more abundant good food, the bright lights of its entertainment world, and the chance to speculate financially. It is significant that China's Guangdong Province, which lies just north of Hong Kong, and especially its provincial capital Canton (Guangzhou), have already outdistanced Shanghai in sophistication and living standards because of this very proximity.

Hong Kong's social problems — such as homelessness and care of the aged — may not be dealt with as soon as the ideas of socialism would seem to dictate in the minds of outsiders. Social care in mainland China is left mainly to family units and pauperdom is common enough. However, it is to be hoped that the Chinese authorities will stop some of the outdated means of geriatric care that are discovered from time to time in Hong Kong. Nor it is not clear whether Hong Kong's huge and numerous charitable organisations will be allowed to continue functioning. With all the contentious issues which Hong Kong and China must face in their unique experiment at combining socialism with capitalism, it is hard to think that Hong Kong will lose all its glitter, wonderful landscapes, or the traditional semi-religious customs which form its peculiar mix of charm and realism.

Hong Kong Island

The brief history of Hong Kong Island is a story of phenomenal growth. When Britain first occupied it in 1841 it was, in Lord Palmerston's much quoted description, 'a barren island with hardly a house upon it'. Today, the island is the centre of one of the most buoyant economies in Asia, with some of the highest population densities in the world.

Hong Kong Island's rapid expansion has consistently astonished the world. The British had been in occupation less than three years when the first governor, Sir Henry Pottinger, reported to England that the settlement had made 'extraordinary and unparalleled progress'. By 1846 the population had doubled (to 24,000, of which 600 were Europeans) and a colonial life-style had evolved: horse-racing had started in Happy Valley, amateur dramatics were underway and the Hong Kong Club was founded. Central was the first area to be developed, with unsanitary, over-crowded Chinese settlements to the east and west of it. Despite continuing bouts of plague and cholera, by the 1870s sinologist the Reverend James Legge spoke of the northern shore's imposing terraces and magnificent residences, and congratulated the Colony on its triumph over the difficulties of its position. Travellers marvelled at the 'Englishness' of the houses and gardens while a guide book extolled the island's magnificent public buildings and hotels. By the turn of the century the population of 300,000 had spread haphazardly from Western to Shaukeiwan and crept up to Mid-levels and the Peak. It seemed controlled urban planning and legislation, even in these early days, never quite kept up with the developers.

With the leasing of the New Territories in 1898, renewed confidence in the Colony meant the injection of more public money into constructing reservoirs and reclaiming more land. The south side became more accessible when work on the first road to encircle the whole island began in 1915.

The rocky scrub-covered mountainous terrain, reminding many a British expatriate of Scotland's rugged west coast, looks wholly unsuited to accommodating persistent waves of immigrants. Yet today the 29-square-mile island has a population of 1.2 million. Most building has been constricted to the flat, narrow strip along the northern shore, and to small areas around Aberdeen, Repulse Bay and Stanley, spreading with extreme difficulty up steep slopes into chiselled-out terraces, or onto land reclaimed from the sea. To the unaccustomed eye, it seems that every possible building site has been exploited to the last square foot. Yet engineers continue to do the impossible, driving four-lane highways through mountains and constructing immense concrete platforms up near-vertical slopes to create yet more building space. While the urban concentrations of Hong Kong Island are now notorious, the beauties of the countryside are less well known. The visitor who ignores the south of the island misses some of the Colony's most spectacular views, some stunning walks, and countryside that combines subtropical vegetation and wild life with open scrub-land, some of it only minutes from Central.

Visitors to Hong Kong Island can experience with relative ease its extraordinary, intensely concentrated blend of oriental and occidental, of urban and rural, of unsightly poverty and ostentatious wealth, of a nostalgic past and an aggressively modern present.

Central

The Central District of Victoria, usually simply known as Central, is the traditional heart of Hong Kong. It was one of the first areas of the 'barren island' to be developed, and today is the centre of Hong Kong's commercial life. Behind concrete and reflecting glass thrives the Territory's big business — finance, trade, banking. At lower levels elegant stores in air-conditioned shopping arcades serve a cosmopolitan clientele. During office hours, the whole area hums with aggressive activity; at night it empties.

There is much of Manhattan in Central's concentrated jumble of highrise blocks which grow almost visibly in a frenetic race to maximise land use. Down below ambitious crowds surge through the streets often spilling off pavements during lunch hour. The jostling pedestrian flow pauses only at windows displaying the latest stockmarket prices or at the lift lobbies when office staff all try to go back to work at the same time.

The first colonisers established in Central a pattern of rapid uncontrolled development that has barely been broken since. Within months of the British flag-raising in January 1841, a track along the coastline had become **Queen's Road** — still the district's main thoroughfare. European traders, including names familiar in China trading such as Jardine and Dent, grabbed lumps of shoreline for their godowns (warehouses) and almost at once began to expand their territory by filling up sections of Victoria Harbour.

The reclamation process has continually altered the shape of the area ever since. By 1860 enough land had been reclaimed to build another waterfront road — **Des Voeux Road** — running parallel to Queen's Road. **Connaught Road** became the third parallel waterfront

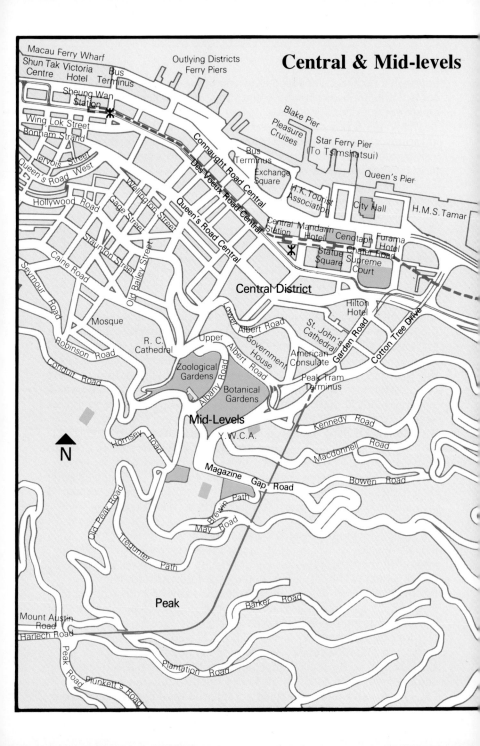

road in 1887, a pet project of Sir Paul Chater, the grand old man of Hong Kong real estate and the co-founder of the giant property developers Hongkong Land.

Few city centres can have experienced so many rapid changes in appearance as Central, where the tradition of tearing down buildings at short intervals to replace them with bigger ones is deeply entrenched. Early photos of Des Voeux Road show elegant slightly Mediterranean three-storey buildings with verandahs shaded by hanging bamboo blinds. Queen's Road had an exotic oriental look about it, packed with pigtailed men and rickshaws, flanked by colonnades of stores, the pillars strung with bold Chinese characters. (A few buildings in this style remain, in Queen's Road West and Queen's Road East.)

Very few of the old buildings and little of the traditional Orient remain. Those buildings which have survived are in active use — there has been no place for sentimentality for the past. As incomes and exports increase, so does the scale of the buildings. To office workers today it must seem that construction sites, pneumatic drills and pile-drivers are a permanent way of life.

Central's rich history exists in a less obvious way, not so much in the fabric of the buildings, but in the names of the streets, stores and buildings. **Pedder Street**, was called after Lt W. Pedder, RN, a harbour master appointed by Captain Elliot. **D'Aguilar Street** is named after Major-General D'Aguilar, the first Commander-in-Chief of the army in Hong Kong. Duddell was a notorious businessman, Pottinger the Colony's first governor, Captain William Caine, the first magistrate, Bonham, Bowring and Des Voeux all governors. **Ice House Street** of course contained the ice house, which operated twice daily delivery services of American-imported ice until the 1880s, when Hong Kong began to manufacture its own.

Some stores are also reminders of Central's early days. **Lane Crawford** was originally a ship's chandler, a far cry from its present-day status as Hong Kong's most prestigious department store. **Watson's the Chemist** goes back to the 1880s, as does **Kelly and Walsh**, the bookstore in Ice House Street, a publisher of early guidebooks to Hong Kong.

Central is linked to Kowloon by the **Star Ferry** (a subway leads down from Chater Road beside the Mandarin Hotel to the pier) and by the MTR. A bus terminus to the west of the Star Ferry is a convenient place to pick up buses for all parts of the island.

At the heart of Central is **Statue Square**, an open area cut into two unequal parts by Chater Road. The Square is virtually unrecognisable from the days when it was edged by ornate white-washed Colonial-style buildings, each topped with cupolas and turrets and encircled by tiers of enclosed verandahs behind Corinthian columns and bulbous balustrades. The design of today's square, with its angular layout of covered sitting areas, rectangles of water and organised tree clusters, was finished in 1966. Today, there is only one statue here — that of Sir Thomas Jackson, chief manager of the Hongkong and Shanghai Bank, 1876—1902. On the north side of Chater Road, a simple cenotaph commemorates the dead of both world wars. On the east is the domed and colonnaded old **Supreme Court**, which in 1985 was converted into the home of the Legislative Council and the offices of the Unofficial Members of the Executive and Legislative Councils. This typical piece of Edwardian public architecture (built 1903—11) was designed by Aston Webb, who was also responsible for London's Victoria and Albert Museum, the facade of Buckingham Palace and Admiralty Arch.

A brave expansion scheme recently was carried out by the **Hongkong and Shanghai Bank**, which has occupied the position on the south side of the square since 1865. Demolition of the attractive 1930s block pictured on millions of banknotes took place in the summer of 1981. But the building replacing these famous headquarters was designed to obliterate any momentary regrets with a dazzling display of steel and glass. Architectural correspondents and others say that British architects Foster Associates have given Hong Kong a much needed aesthetic treat with one of the world's most interesting and, at an estimated HK$1.4 billion, most expensive commercial developments.

With 47 levels above ground and four levels below ground, the bank's 600-foot tall headquarters unquestionably dominates its banking neighbours. To the west is the **Chartered Bank**, another established international group. To the east is the chunky grey building of the **Bank of China**, its doorways guarded by solid square-faced Chinese lions. It is through this bank and a network of a dozen or so other China-controlled banks, that Peking holds sway over a sizeable proportion of Hong Kong's bank deposits (some say as high as 20 percent). Aside from housing its banking activities, the building has doubled as Peking's trade, diplomatic and political headquarters. Anywhere else in the world the Bank of China's sombre presence would seem incongruous, with the Hilton behind it, the Hongkong and Shanghai Bank next door, and a last remnant of Edwardian England, the former Supreme Court Building, opposite. But in Hong Kong the peaceful proximity of such contrasts is the norm. And already a 70-storey building is taking shape to the east to house the Bank of China in the grandest possible style. Designed by I.M. Pei, this promises to be yet another fascinating addition to Central's collection of notable buildings.

A little way up Garden Road, past the Hilton, on the right hand side, is the characteristically Victorian **St John's Cathedral** built between 1847−49, with a distinctive square neo-gothic tower. This is the oldest permanent centre of Christian worship in Hong Kong and still the focus of Hong Kong's Anglican community. The first bishop was a missionary, George Smith, who was given a diocese which, with the supreme self-confidence of 19th-century Britain, covered not only Hong Kong but also all of China and Japan. The ravages of white ants led to major restoration work in 1981.

A path from Garden Road leads past St John's Cathedral to a quieter green patch of mature trees and thick subtropical shrubbery. From here **Battery Path** slopes down to Queen's Road Central, past the recently restored red Amoy brick former French Mission. The building, which dates back to the 1880s, has a versatile past, at different times housing government departments, the Hongkong and Shanghai Bank junior mess, Butterfield and Swire, the Russian Consulate and, of course, the French Mission.

The section of Queen's Road Central from Ice House Street to Pedder Street is dominated by massive construction activity — all part of giant property developers Hongkong Land's scheme for reshaping Central. Hongkong Land are masters of the art of acquiring, pulling down and putting up property in Central. But the current plan exceeds all past efforts and includes covered walkways between their properties. It is now possible to walk from Queen's Road to the MTR or Star Ferry without touching street level. The centre of this scheme is the **Landmark**, with its elegant window displays of chic, international stores. Eighty or so banks, airline offices, restaurants, jewellers and boutiques are housed here. Inside the Landmark, a vast air-conditioned hall incorporates the latest fashions in public indoor plazas. Escalators sail up past murals to suspended balconies; fountains disport themselves in a circular pool; and overhead a kinetic glass fibre sculpture vibrates to light. At times the fountain in the high atrium is switched off and a platform is erected over it to stage performances and displays of many kinds.

As you cross Connaught Road from Pedder Street, looking towards the harbour, the brand new 52-storey **Exchange Square** comes into view. It houses the new unified Stock Exchange, stockbrokers and other international firms, as well as a sandwich bar and a number of other eating establishments. Next to it is the massive round-windowed 52-storey **Connaught Centre** built in 1974. Both projects are owned by Hongkong Land, and until the opening of the Hopewell Centre in

Wanchai, Connaught Centre was the tallest building in Hong Kong. Behind it is the **General Post Office** and Government Publications Sales Office, and to the east the Star Ferry pier. Beside the Star Ferry is a wide open promenade, Edinburgh Place, overlooking the harbour, with **City Hall**'s complex of buildings behind. Opened in 1962, these units are the focus of Hong Kong's public artistic life (see Arts, page 56). The Low Block contains a concert hall, a theatre and two restaurants. The 12-storey High Block contains the Museum of Art (see Museums, page 72), an exhibition gallery and art gallery, libraries, lecture halls and the Hong Kong Marriage Registry. The garden below is a favourite spot for photographing newly-weds.

East of the City Hall complex is **HMS Tamar**, the Royal Navy shore base in Hong Kong. The British Armed Forces have always been a dominant presence in Central, and their insistence on retaining large chunks of land and shoreline was a long standing frustration to planners and developers. Today's base — sometimes known as the Stone Frigate, since it is officially classed as a Royal Navy Ship — is all that is left of the old Naval dockyard which before land reclamation stretched eastwards to Wanchai and right up to Victoria Barracks. The Army was housed in Victoria Barracks, first established in 1843, until 1978, when the headquarters moved in with the Navy into the 28-storey Prince of Wales building in the HMS Tamar compound. The tower's narrow base is a security feature, which allows the entire building to be sealed off in an emergency.

Victoria Barracks is to be partially developed: a new 22-storey **Supreme Court Building** comprising a six-storey podium and a 16-storey tower block housing 36 court rooms and ancillary accommodation was completed in 1984. The old Flagstaff House, now the **Flagstaff House Museum of Tea Ware**, is one of the finest remaining colonial buildings in Hong Kong (see Museums, page 72).

Five minutes' walk up from Queen's Road Central is **Government House**, the residence of the Governor. Entry is forbidden but it is possible to look through the main gate in Upper Albert Road at the sweeping drive and facade. The building started life as a square neo-classical structure put up in 1855−56 under the watchful eye of Cleverly, a surveyor-general of Hong Kong. Considerable alterations and additions have since been made, the most incongruous of which is the prominent quasi-oriental tower constructed by the Japanese, who occupied Government House during the Second World War. The Japanese were also responsible for lengthening the roof corners, which are curved upwards and outwards, and for the portico.

One Sunday a year, in spring, when the garden's magnificent azaleas are in bloom, the grounds are opened to the public. This is an immensely popular event and queues form several hours before the gates open. Opposite Government House are the **Botanical and Zoological Gardens**, well worth a visit for anyone seeking a pleasant subtropical leafy retreat. The tiny gardens were created on the terraced hillside in 1860, and since then the varied lush vegetation has made them a favourite with residents. If you go early in the morning you can watch people going through their *tai chi* exercises. On a fine Sunday it is a popular place for family outings.

The small zoo boasts an outstanding collection of birds, including many rarities like the Palawan peacock from the Philippines. The relatively small collection of mammals (orang-utans, monkeys, jaguars) still attracts more visitors than London Zoo — although entry here of course is free. You can enter from Garden Road, Albany Road, Glenealy or Robinson Road. The gardens are divided in two by Albany Road, the two halves linked by an underground walkway.

The Peak

As orientation for the first-time visitor to Hong Kong, or for the sheer delight of the views, nothing can beat a trip up Hong Kong Island's highest mountain, Victoria Peak.

Since the 1870s, when the Governor Sir Richard Macdonnell took to spending the hot and humid months in his summer residence on the Peak, the area has become the enclave of Hong Kong's richest and most influential inhabitants. Many elegant houses are scattered over the slopes of Mount Kellet, Victoria Peak itself and Mount Gough, where the temperatures are lower but the social position is higher. Up here (said a 19th-century traveller), 'one can spend the summer in Hong Kong with a reasonable probability of being alive at the end of it'.

In the early days access to the Peak was only on foot or by sedan chair, but since 1888 the eight-minute ride on the Peak Tram has taken much of the effort out of the 396-metre (1,302-foot) climb. The Number 15 bus from Central offers a longer (30–40 minute) but no-less-scenic route to the top.

Public transport terminates at the **Peak Tower** which lies in the saddle between surrounding mountains. From the viewing platform or restaurants here there are splendid panoramic views of the northern shore of the island, across the harbour to Kowloon and Kai Tak Airport. In the opposite direction the southern side of Hong Kong Island comes into view across Aberdeen to Lamma, Lantau and the South China Sea. Many fine walks begin from the Peak Tower

114

Shelley Street Mosque above Caine Road was the first founded in Hong Kong. The present structure dates from 1916.

complex. One of the easiest and most satisfying is the 45-minute stroll round Victoria Peak along Harlech Road and Lugard Road where you can get unprecedented views of the city, sea and Outlying Islands.

Western

For a taste of the traditional life of Hong Kong, there is no better place to go than Western District — to the outsider an exotic, crowded area extending westward from Central that combines the picturesque with the squalid. It is an old residential and commercial area of narrow streets with crumbling three-storey buildings, hawkers' stalls and small wholesale outlets.

It was in Western that the British flag was first hoisted in January 1841. The event is commemorated in the name of a narrow, unprepossessing street, **Possession Point** (not worth a special visit), and until recently by a small square surrounded by tumble down houses. New high-rise blocks and a covered hawkers' bazaar, painted in lurid turquoise, have now been put up in the square.

But there are still several chunks of Western that are appealing for a glimpse of traditional urban Chinese life. Walk from Central or take a tram along Des Voeux Road to **Western Market**, a handsome old building in deep red Amoy brick. Turn up into **Morrison Street**, part of an asymmetrical jumble of streets lined with fruit and vegetable stalls. On the left a herbalist sells two kinds of invigorating drinks — one dark and bitter and the other light and sweet. On the corner of **Bonham Strand**, several shops sell traditional everyday wood, rattan and bamboo ware — ginger graters, rattan pillows, wok brushes, fans and washboards. This is also the area for snake shops. At No 91 Bonham Strand the reptiles are kept in smart wooden boxes, fitted ceiling to floor, with red and gold plush. No 127 is more downmarket, with snakes quite visible in wire cages. In **Mercier Street**, amidst sellers of fishing tackle, string and tropical fish, is the Chinese Gold and Silver Exchange — a small insignificant looking building which does not allow spectators in, although even a glimpse through the door gives a lasting impression of the frenetic activity inside.

Further west towards **Sai Ying Pun**, the banks and general stores of Des Voeux Road give way to ship chandlers and wholesalers and retailers selling a bewildering array of dried fish imported from China, Japan and Korea. There are shark's fins of all qualities, the best often kept behind glass and priced at over HK$500 a catty (about 1.25 lbs). Some of the dried merchandise is recognisable — whole fish, shrimps, oysters, snake (hung in large single oils) and squid. Others are less so. The brown one-inch discs in jars, for instance, are pieces cut from a

scallop's root muscle, and the yellowish papery squares are jelly fish with tentacles removed. Other stores specialise in dried mushrooms, including an expensive, crinkly off-white fungus which expands dramatically when soaked and is good for a clear complexion, and the popular 'cloud ear' which looks like scraps of charred paper until it is cooked, when it takes on the shape of an elephant's ear. Sacks of tangerine peel, red-brown melon seeds, dried lotus seeds, preserved bean-curd and much else also turn up in these shops.

Moving inland from here up **Centre** or **Eastern Street**, across Queen's Road West, the streets become very busy with markets selling Chinese vegetables, herbs, fruit, sweets, chickens and quails. At right angles First, Second and Third streets are characteristic of old residential Western, the houses adorned with a tangle of curved wrought iron balconies, pot plants, shrines, washing, wire-netting and bird cages.

Back eastwards a few blocks, the tiny streets around **Tai Ping Shan** (north of Hollywood Road) are interesting. This area was the site of a Chinese settlement before Hong Kong was ceded to the British (Tai Ping Shan, or Mountain of Peace, was the Chinese name for Victoria Peak). The early settlers were said to be followers of a notorious pirate who controlled the waters around Hong Kong at the end of the 18th century. Later, when the number of Chinese immigrants increased as the British settled in, the area became an important, densely-populated, highly unhealthy commercial and residential centre. The original buildings were torn down and rebuilt at the end of the century after a particularly bad bubonic plague epidemic, but many of today's houses seem little altered from that period.

Three small temples stand in **Tai Ping Shan Street**. The surrounding steep lanes, narrow alleyways and steps paved with smooth stones are a mass of accompanying paraphernalia — joss-sticks, paper offerings to be burnt, and fortune tellers. On the corner with Pound Lane are the **Temples of Kuan-yin** and **Sui-tsing Paak**, their origins going back to 1840. Women whose children are ill, or who have other domestic problems, flock to Kuan-yin. The General Sui-tsing Paak next door is believed to cure sickness. Several other gods are included in this temple, the sea-goddess Tin Hau among them. An interesting hall has 60 images, each dedicated to one year of the Chinese 60-year cycle. Another has a replica of the mummified body of Hui Neng, founder of the Buddhist Vegetarian Sect. Outside is a much used open shrine to Earth Gods, who protect the local community. The third temple is the **Paak Sing**, first established in 1851 (and rebuilt in 1895), to house tablets dedicated to the dead. The inner room contains over 3,000 tablets (and photographs). Temple keepers burn incense and oil lamps in front of the tablets for a small fee.

Walking back towards Central you come across Hong Kong's famous ladder streets. The Cantonese equivalent of 'stair street' is in fact more appropriate for these narrow steep stone staircases. The most spectacular is **Ladder Street** itself, which climbs 213 feet up from its junction with Hollywood Road to Caine Road. There is a considerably shorter equivalent in Central — Pottinger Street — lined with sellers of buttons and bows, sewing cottons, shoes, combs and other haberdashery.

Hollywood Road and **Cat Street** (Upper Lascar Road) have lost much of their character under an urban renewal scheme (though not their antique shops nor Cat Street's flea market). The **Man Mo Temple**, 126 Hollywood Road — a fine example of a Taoist temple built on traditional lines — is well worth a visit if you are in the area. It is heavily used by worshippers who carry on apparently oblivious to the large number of tourists who go there. The temple is dedicated to two Taoist deities — Man Cheong, the god of literature, who also looks after civil servants, and Mo Kwan Kung, the martial god who, it is said, represents the qualities of the two influential Chinese community leaders who founded the temple in 1842. It was rebuilt in 1894.

Behind the fire screening door at the main entrance, the atmosphere is thick with smoke from the giant incense coils that hang in profusion from the ceiling of the section known as 'the smoke tower'. The coils, which burn for two weeks, are ideal for long term offerings. The worshipper's prayers are written on the red tag that hangs from each. Below, paper offerings are burnt in the two stone incinerators and, on the other side, stand symbols of the Eight Immortals.

On the long marble-topped table at the top of the steps that lead to the main section (or palace) are two solid brass deer standing about three feet high, symbolising long life. And on the table in front of the main altar is a fine set of pewter *Ng Kung*, or five ritual vessels, as well as a central incense burner, a pair of vases and candlesticks on either side.

On the main shrine, Man Cheong (on the left) and Mo Kwan Kung (on the right) sit together. To the right is the shrine to the City God, Shing Wang, who looks after city dwellers, and to the left is Pao Kung, the God of Justice. The temple was in fact used early on as a Chinese Court to judge disputes amongst the Chinese community. Also in the temple are three finely-carved, teak sedan chairs which until recently were used to carry the statues of Man and Mo through the street during festivals. The drum and bell (cast in Canton in 1847) are on the right hand wall. In the adjoining All Saints Temple a soothsayer waits to tell you what the gods have in store for you.

Wanchai

Wanchai is associated in most people's minds with Suzie Wong, sailors
and lurid, neon-lit nightlife (see Nightlife). But for anyone prepared to
explore on foot, there is far more to this interesting old district, which
was one of the five original *wan*, the areas set aside for the Chinese
population who arrived on Hong Kong Island during the 1850s.

Wanchai was once a stretch of waterfront along Queen's Road
East, but early this century reclamation provided new space for
Wanchai's characteristic three- and four-storey tenements, with ground
floor stores and residential quarters above, that spread as far as
Gloucester Road, the 1930s waterline. Today there is another broad
strip of reclaimed land on the north side of Gloucester Road, which is
gradually filling up with new highrise office blocks, a sportsground, the
Arts Centre and the APA (see Arts, page 56), and a ferry pier.

The face of pre-war Wanchai is rapidly disappearing as developers
take over in this frenzy of office-block construction. The tallest of these
is the **Hopewell Centre**, which rises an improbable 66 storeys out of
Queen's Road East. Apart from restaurants on floors six to eight, the
revolving restaurant on top and two shopping floors, the whole
cylindrical building is taken up by office space — a daring and highly-
successful venture by a local developer born and bred in Wanchai.

The Hopewell is incongruously surrounded by several historical
sites. Almost next door is the tiny Wanchai post office, one of the
area's few protected remnants from the last century. A little closer to
Central is the single-storeyed **Hung Shing Temple** dedicated to a god of
seafarers. A shrine inside is dated 1847−8, although the building was
constructed in 1860. The splendid line of Shekwan pottery decorating
the roof was added at the turn of the century. On the other side of the
Hopewell Centre, a picturesque alley with its name, Tik Loong Lane,
written over the entrance, leads up steps to a crumbling terrace of
19th-century houses. Several of these incorporate the **Sui Pak Temple**,
which was probably founded in the 1870s and is especially popular with
people wanting medical help. The interior contains many mirrors
inscribed by grateful worshippers who have recovered from illnesses.
Upstairs is an interesting collection of antiques.

In the narrow side streets that lead into Queen's Road East you
may stumble over traditional shops selling birds, crickets, snakes or
fragile brightly coloured paper offerings. Fortune tellers, traditional
hairdressers and professional letter-writers have set up their tables on
the pavements hereabouts. **Wanchai Market**, which runs from Queen's
Road East down Wanchai Road is one of the most interesting to
wander through (go around 9 am−11 am, or in the late afternoon).

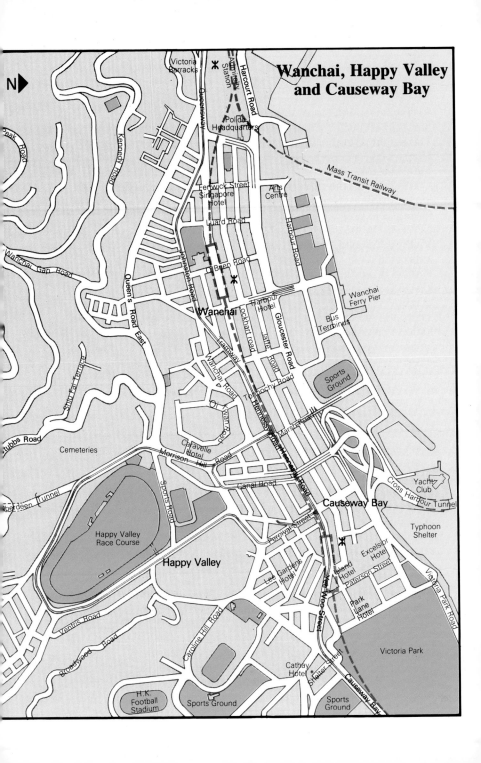

Happy Valley

Racing began in Happy Valley in 1845 and has been one of the major preoccupations for Chinese and expatriates ever since (see Sports). The height of enthusiasm was perhaps reached when Governor Sir Henry May, a keen horse-owner, took to the track as a jockey with some success.

Aside from the racecourse, Happy Valley, once swampy and malaria-ridden, is now a pleasant residential area, which first became fashionable in the 1870s when the wealthy began to move away from Central. On the south side of the race-track is an entrance to Happy Valley's **Colonial Cemetery**, established in 1845. It can also be approached via another entrance much higher on Stubbs Road. Amidst flowering trees and well-kept hillside gardens (the setting for a key scene in John Le Carre's *The Honourable Schoolboy*), the gravestones vividly bring to life much of Hong Kong's early history. There are graves bearing British, Russian, German, and Chinese names. The many monuments include one to the American officers and crew who died in a boat attack on a fleet of piratical junks in 1855, one in memory of a French crew which disappeared in a typhoon in 1906, and of course many to the British soldiers and their families who died of fever. The new Aberdeen Tunnel emerges nearby.

Causeway Bay

Wanchai merges imperceptibly into Causeway Bay, the busy area most favoured by locals for shopping and eating. Innumerable restaurants, jewellers, camera shops, boutiques and electrical stores mingle with the largest China Products store in Hong Kong, three big Japanese department stores, a branch of Lane Crawford, several shopping malls as well as a few garment factory outlets in the back streets behind the Excelsior Hotel. Prices throughout are better than in Central, and the area is often thronged with shoppers taking advantage of the range of goods and the late closing hours (9 or 10 pm).

Trading is not new to Causeway Bay. The most famous *hong* (trading house), Jardine, Matheson & Company Limited, set up shop here in 1841. Jardine's most famous relic is the Noon-Day Gun, made known to the world by Noel Coward's 'Mad Dogs and Englishmen':

'In Hong Kong they strike a gong
And fire off a noonday gun.'

Causeway Bay long ago lost its bay to extensive reclamation, although it still has a **typhoon shelter**, where on summer nights (between April and November) you can enjoy a floating dinner. Hire a sampan on the waterfront (most easily reached via the pedestrian bridge from Victoria Park) to take you out into the shelter. The food (not cheap) is chosen from the boats that cluster round the sampan, and for extra dollars a music boat will serenade you.

One bonus of the reclamation completed some 30 years ago is **Victoria Park**. Opened in 1957, the 7.7-hectare (19-acre) park is not especially beautiful, but it is an interesting and accessible place for an insight into Hong Kong's early morning life. (Between 6 and 7.30 am is the best time to go.) Under clumps of trees, you can see groups of people of all ages go slowly through their *tai chi ch'uan* exercises. Impressively fit individuals practise various forms of *kung fu* while others jog round the flat central grass area. Bird cages are hung in the trees to give the birds an airing while their owners chat below. The park is heavily used throughout the day. It has swimming pools, mini-soccer pitches, tennis and basketball courts, but has recently lost some land to the MTR for construction of a new station.

A bizarre park of another kind is **Tiger Balm Gardens**, a place which is much maligned but offers a fascinating view of Buddhist mythology and Chinese taste. The founder, Aw Boon Haw, was a Chinese millionaire philanthropist who made his money with the most famous of cure-alls, Tiger Balm, used for asthma, lumbago, sore throat, scorpion bites and much else.

The garden was built in 1935 on eight acres of very steep hillside behind Causeway Bay. Grotesque and amusing plaster figures depicting Chinese folktales or Buddhist stories ornament every ledge and corner. Most lurid (and furthest to climb) are those representing the *Ten Courts of Hell*. There is also a monument to Aw's parents and a decorative Tiger Pagoda, with 149 steps up its six storeys. The gardens are open daily from 9 am to 4 pm. The Aw family's jade collection was scheduled to open to the public in May 1988.

North Point and Shaukeiwan

East from Causeway Bay to North Point, Quarry Bay and Shaukeiwan, population density and industry intensify. These areas are for anyone who wants to see something of Hong Kong's industrial life or low-cost housing estates. **North Point**, or 'little Shanghai', because of all the Shanghainese who have settled there, is an oppressive mass of 1960s residential blocks, vast restaurants, street markets and heavy traffic.

Quarry Bay is the oldest industrial area in Hong Kong — ship building began here with the establishment of Whampoa Dock in 1863. The Taikoo Dockyard, founded by Butterfield and Swire, was in full operation in 1908. Today much of it has been redeveloped as a large private housing estate — Taikoo Shing — while the remaining yards are operated by a joint concern, the Hong Kong United Dockyard Company.

Shaukeiwan was for a long time a small fishing village, persistently bothered by pirates, the most notorious of whom was based on the mainland opposite at Lei Yu Mun. This is the shortest stretch of water to the mainland, and the one the Japanese used when invading Hong Kong Island. Today the crossing can be made by public ferry to eat at one of Lei Yu Mun's seafood restaurants (see New Territories).

Shaukeiwan today is the base of Hong Kong's second largest fishing fleet (Aberdeen's is bigger), and a densely populated residential area. The traditional art of junk building carries on in **Aldrich Bay**, but there is much new industry as well. If you have time to spare, visit the **Tin Hau Temple** opposite the fish market, or the interesting **Tam Kung Temple**. Tam Kung, with his ability to heal the sick and control the weather, became the boat community's second-ranking patron deity after Tin Hau. His festival, on the eighth day of the fourth moon, is one of the island's most spectacular celebrations. Boats carrying shrines come from all over Hong Kong, offerings are made, and dragon and lion dances are performed.

Repulse Bay and Stanley

No perspective of Hong Kong Island would be complete without making the easy trip to the south side of the island. Until 1920 when a road to Repulse Bay was completed, the fishing settlements at Repulse Bay and Stanley were small and isolated, accessible only by a narrow track, or by boat. Today there is a constant stream of traffic to these now popular residential areas, served by regular buses and plenty of taxis. The route along Stubbs Road and Wongneichong Gap Road winds above Happy Valley racecourse, and crosses over to the greener side of the island. The road curls down steep slopes past smart houses and residential blocks in leafy settings, with superb views across to **Deep Water Bay** (where there is a pleasant though crowded beach), Ocean Park and Lamma Island. In off-peak traffic it takes half an hour from Central to Repulse Bay and another ten minutes on to Stanley.

The sandy, shallow **Repulse Bay** got its name from 19th-century pirate-chaser, the *HMS Repulse*. For some the name has strong colonial associations, largely because of the famous old **Repulse Bay Hotel** which was built in 1918. It was demolished to make way for a high-rise development, but a replica of the original restaurant has been built. It is the site of the island's most accessible beach, which unsurprisingly is also its most heavily used.

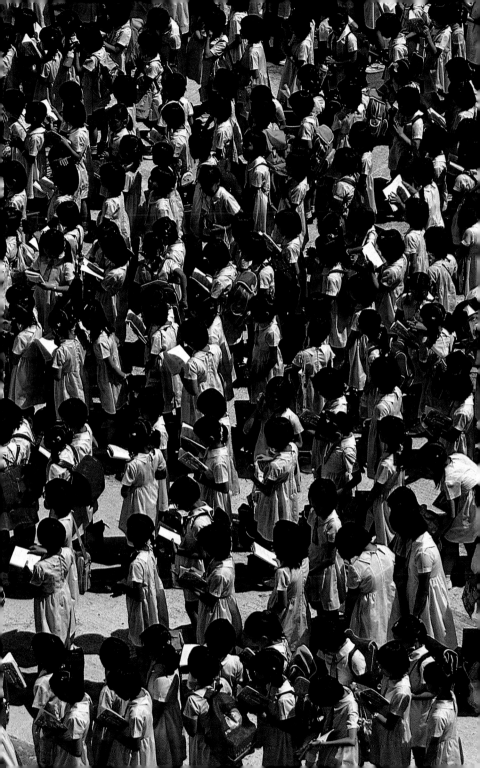

The road through Repulse Bay winds on towards **Stanley**, passing more glorious views, and more elegant residences. Stanley had the largest population (some 2,000 people) of any settlement on the island when the British arrived in 1841, but did not develop until the 1920s when the island road reached it. The village has strong military associations. Part of the headland, first set aside for Army use in the 1930s, is still a restricted Army base. Stanley was the scene of the most heroic, and inevitably hopeless, resistance to the Japanese invasion in December 1941, and it was here that many of Hong Kong's civilians were herded together in a camp, now Stanley Prison, until the Japanese surrender in August 1945.

Most visitors to Stanley these days are in search of bargains in the small market. Bundles of jeans, T-shirts, sweaters and jackets, as well as silk dresses and suits, are stacked unceremoniously on stalls and sold at ridiculously low prices, taking all the glamour out of the (not always genuine) designer labels. Small rattan and porcelain shops cater increasingly to tourists, whose recent influx has led to a rise in prices and a general smartening up of the narrow pedestrian market street.

Yet despite the influx, Stanley village is still a pleasant place to spend a couple of hours. If you go by bus, get off at the small grassy triangle and walk down Stanley Market Street which slopes towards the fruit and vegetable market. On the right is a small fish market (best in the morning) and food stalls which cook the fish you buy for yourself in the market. To find the market (situated where there is a China Products shop) turn left off Market Street. If you feel like a swim, **Stanley's main beach**, facing Tai Tam Bay, is five minutes away past the bus stop. There is also an interesting **Tin Hau Temple** at the other end of the village, thought to be around 200 years old and so the oldest on the island. Turn right at the bottom of Stanley Market Road into Stanley Main Street and walk along the promenade past the squatter huts to the temple where a statue of Tin Hau, the Queen of Heaven and guardian of all connected with the sea, stands looking out across the ocean.

The unpretentious temple has much in common with Hong Kong's other Tin Hau temples. But one unusual feature is the four-foot high stone ledge, which runs round three walls of the main hall and carries an awesome array of black and gold gods thought to date back some 200 years. On the wall to the left of the altar, look for the dirty skin of a tiger said to have been shot only a hundred yards from the temple by Japanese soldiers during the occupation of Hong Kong.

Shek O

Shek O, although today largely occupied by commuters, still has the air of an unkempt Cantonese village about it. The countrified surroundings include a large golf course and even a few vegetable farms. It is not easily accessible from Central: take a Number 9 bus from Shaukeiwan (about 30 minutes) or a taxi from Central (off-peak 50 minutes). At weekends the village attracts large crowds, but on weekdays the wide sandy beach is emptier, and a walk through the warren of narrow pedestrian streets around a tiny Tin Hau Temple gives a glimpse of a lifestyle far removed from the dense urban living on the island's north shore. Good plain Cantonese food is served in several simple restaurants. Walk through the village along the main street to reach Shek O Headland, bordered by luxury houses, and go down a footbridge across to the tiny rocky island of Tin Tau Chau. In 10 minutes you can climb up the cemented path to a lookout position with splendid views north to Joss House Bay and the mainland, and south to Stanley Peninsula with a satellite communications station at its tip and the Po Toi Island group in the distance.

Ocean Park

Around two million visitors a year flock to Ocean Park, understandably one of the most popular places for Hong Kong families to spend a morning or an afternoon. After more than 10 years of feasibility studies and construction, it opened in January, 1977, and since then many additional features have been added. The 65-hectare (160-acre) park is set in rocky terrain just east of Aberdeen; the lowland and headland areas are linked by cable car and by escalator. The lowland area is the home of Water World, which has giant slides, a wave pool, a rapids ride and a toddlers' pool. The playpark adds further variety to the lowland area's already extensive attractions, which include an Omnimax Cinema, a zoo, children's playground, goldfish exhibition, dolphin feeding pools, a garden theatre where regular entertainment is given by sea lions and other animals, and a plaza area, where trained cockatoos and macaws entertain.

But it is the spectacular seven-minute ride to the headland in six-seater gondola cars high above the rocky slopes which makes the visit worthwhile. On the headland itself is the world's largest marine mammal tank and the world's largest aquarium. The Ocean Theatre with its panoramic backdrop holds 4,000 people and stages performances by dolphins, sea-lions and a killer whale compered by a remarkable bilingual master of ceremonies.

The vast Atoll Reef, a seawater aquarium, holds 200 different species of fish which swim around in an enormous tank that has been designed to give the impression of a coral reef. Viewing galleries take the visitor down from the shallow upper reef levels to depths normally reserved for deep sea divers. A Wave Cove with 328 feet of 'coastline' and a unique wave-making machine is a splendid home for sea-lions, seals and penguins and can also be viewed from an underwater gallery. The entrance to Ocean Park is located opposite the southern end of the Aberdeen Tunnel.

Aberdeen

The old fishing town of Aberdeen traditionally has been included on the Hong Kong Island tourist route. But recent changes have been so sweeping that many visitors feel it is hardly worth a special visit. The area is fast developing into an urban-industrial district to equal North Point, Quarry Bay and Shaukeiwan. Reclamation of the harbour has all but destroyed the old character of the waterfront, although, apparently undeterred, the boat people still sell their fresh catch to passers-by and noisy sampan ladies tout for custom. The famous floating restaurants were moved away from the waterfront in 1978 to less spectacular moorings in a secluded part of the typhoon anchorage. On shore, the centre of the town is now a western-style shopping complex surrounded by high-rise resettlement blocks.

For a fine overview of the harbour you can climb up some steps onto the Ap Lei Chau Bridge pedestrian walkway. The bridge, opened in 1979, enabled the 20th century to spill onto this tiny island, which earlier had existed entirely on its flourishing ship-building industry.

For boat enthusiasts, the shipyards around Ap Lei Chau are a paradise. Many kinds of small craft are built here including, of course, junks, which are still constructed by skilled carpenters who today have added electric drills to their traditional tool kits. Diesel engines, which have replaced the picturesque sails, are repaired here. Scrap iron and steel from ships broken up here are converted into metal products used in the construction industry.

The disfiguring five-chimney electric power station that dominates the island provides power for much of Hong Kong Island. It will shortly be closed down and the land on which it stands redeveloped.

Because of the large boat population, Aberdeen's Tin Hau Temple is heavily used. It was built in 1851 on what was then the shoreline; but today it is in the centre of town set in a small garden. The bell on the left as you enter the temple was made in 1726 and reputedly dredged up from the sea by local fishermen. The one on the right dates from

1851. A statue of Tin Hau sits in the central shrine with a smaller image of her in front (this is carried out of the temple at festivals). Two almost life-size generals stand in front of her — Thousand-Li Eye on the left, who could see a thousand *li* (300 miles), and Favourable Wind Ear on the right, who could hear distinctly up to a thousand *li* away. To Tin Hau's left and right are shrines to Pi Tai who fought the demon king barefoot, wearing a black robe.

Kowloon

Little is known of Kowloon's early history, though the Lei Cheng Uk
tomb (see Museums, page 72) in Lai Chi Kok just north of Kowloon is
evidence of Eastern Han Dynasty (25–220) settlers. In 1277 the Sung
Dynasty's last emperor, Ti Ping, and his brother, Ti Ching, under the
guardianship of their uncle, Yang Liang-chieh, found refuge in
Kowloon. The Mongol army from which they were fleeing had
captured and disposed of their eldest brother, the former emperor, and
taken the Southern Dynasty's capital of Hangchow. On arrival in
Kowloon, a temporary court was set up near the present airport. Here
the eight-year-old emperor and his brother are said to have spent many
hours playing in the shadow of a great rock overlooking the sea. Some
years later the rock was engraved with the message 'Sung Wong Toi'
(Terrace of the Sung Emperor). Sadly, during the Japanese
Occupation in the Second World War it was broken up to make way
for the Kai Tak runway though a fragment bearing the inscription was
saved and can be seen today in the **Sung Wong Toi Garden**.

On his arrival the young emperor asked the name of his new home
and was told that it was Kowloon, meaning 'nine dragons' after the
peaks in the ridge of hills which lie behind it. Dragons are a traditional
symbol of imperial majesty and are believed to inhabit mountain
ridges. When the boy remarked that he could only see eight — today
there are fewer as some have fallen foul of the developers' dynamite —
he was told that he, the emperor, was the ninth.

The next major event in Kowloon's recorded history was in 1860
when it was ceded to Britain following the Second Opium War. In
1895 Kowloon was described by the traveller, Henry Norman, as the
'ground floor' of the Colony, Mid-levels being the 'second storey' and
the Peak the 'top storey'. In other words Kowloon was one of the
mercantile centres, Mid-levels was for executive living, with the Peak
for the *tai pans* (bosses). This is very much the feeling of Kowloon
today — a bustling market place.

The Kowloon Peninsula is surrounded by one of the most
breathtaking and vibrant scenes in the world — **Victoria Harbour**, with
the startling backdrop of mountainous Hong Kong (Victoria) Island
and its multitude of buildings, some climbing precariously up to the
Peak. This perfect natural harbour of 23 square miles is a constant hive
of activity. It plays host to all manner of craft — aged junks from the
mainland propelled majestically by great patched sails; jetfoils and
hydrofoils plying between Hong Kong and Macau; the more sedate
lozenge-shaped Star ferries; the numerous Hong Kong Yaumatei
Ferries serving the Outlying Islands; sleek warships; container vessels

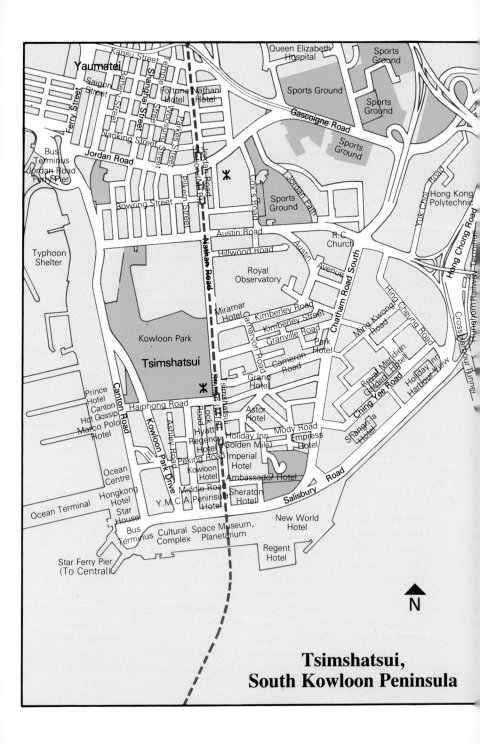

**Tsimshatsui,
South Kowloon Peninsula**

and bulk cargo carriers; tugs and lighters; police launches and every imaginable type of pleasure vessel. Once a year the liner *Queen Elizabeth II* docks at Ocean Terminal. In 1842 a total of 381 vessels used the harbour; in 1986 the figure was 95,200. In 1987 Hong Kong officially overtook Rotterdam to become the world's busiest container port. Harbour-watching, a constant pleasure whether from land or sea, was enhanced in 1981 by the completion of a walkway along the waterfront from Kowloon Pier to Hunghom. A night-time crossing on the Star Ferry is particularly spectacular. If you miss the last ferry home (11.30 pm) hire a walla-walla from Blake or Queen's Pier: on one of these small, noisy water taxis you will find yourself caught up in the true fairy-like quality of the harbour at night.

The area of the Kowloon Peninsula is 11 square kilometres (4.3 square miles) stretching north from the waterfront to Boundary Street, which marks the extent of the land ceded, in 1860. Tsimshatsui (a tongue twister pronounced 'Chim Sa Choy') which means 'sharp sand point' is the peninsula's town. Surprisingly many of the neighbouring districts such as Laichikok and the **Walled City of Kowloon** are strictly speaking not in Kowloon proper. The so-called Walled City was built in the 1840s by a group of Chinese who wished to protect themselves from the British 'barbarians'. The walls, like the Sung Wong Toi Rock, disappeared during the Second World War when the Japanese needed stones to build the Kai Tak runway, so today little remains of the old city, an unsanitary slum which is soon to be demolished and turned into a park.

The best way to see the southern part of Tsimshatsui is on foot. If you arrive on the Star Ferry, just prior to docking you will see on the right a fine orange and white clock tower built in 1910 to commemorate the Victoria Jubilee. This is all that remains of the old railway station which was demolished in 1978 to make way for the Cultural Complex. The clock, protected from the wreckers' hammer, has caused certain amusement in the past by occasionally running backwards. Just to the left of the Star Ferry exit is Harbour City, the vast shopping complex formed by **Ocean Terminal** and **Ocean Centre** and other buildings running up Canton Road (see Shopping). In addition to the cornucopia of shops and restaurants, there are occasionally Chinese cultural shows in the main concourse of Ocean Terminal.

Walking along Salisbury Road, in the first block on the left (opposite the bus station) is Star House. On the ground and first floors is a large and well-stocked **Chinese Arts and Crafts Store** (see Shopping). On the second floor is the **Chinese Export Commodities Exhibition Hall**, which is mainland China's showcase for displays of archaeological treasures or products ranging from tractors to exquisite silk embroidery. Often there are visiting craftsmen demonstrating how handicrafts are made in different provinces.

Leaving Star House, continue walking east past the imposing portico of the **YMCA**. On the opposite side of the street is the **Space Museum** and site of the **Cultural Complex** (see Museums). Walking further along Salisbury Road you pass the venerable Peninsula Hotel (see Hotels). Turn left up **Nathan Road**, main artery of Kowloon. This three-mile, tree-lined boulevard was built at the turn of the century during the governorship of Sir Mathew Nathan. At the time sceptics dubbed it Nathan's Folly: what possible use, they asked, could this boulevard serve in a sparsely populated, unfashionable area? However, times have changed and the southernmost mile is a densely populated, highly commercial area considered the prime beat of shoppers. The streets to the right and left offer a host of diversions, in fact nearly anything anyone could desire (see Shopping and Nightlife).

One of the newer sights in Kowloon, opened in 1979, is a replica of a **Sung Dynasty Village** (AD 960−1279). This is a sensitive and faithful re-creation of one of the richest cultural periods of China's history. Chinese garden architects have always dealt with small spaces very effectively, allowing the visitor to see only limited sections of an area at any one time, thereby creating the illusion of greater size. To some extent this 60,000-square-foot village follows this concept. The overall plan is a rectangle, edged with buildings and a picturesque stream bordered by open-fronted shops and mature trees. Once inside the great entrance gate the tour begins in earnest. First comes a monkey show, then a contemporary weapons display in the village tower, followed by calls at quaint stream-side shops where, with the help of the Sung paper money coupons handed out on arrival, one can buy sesame seed cookies and a longed-for cup of jasmine tea while listening to musicians accompanying a young singer. All the villagers are dressed in Sung costume, in which they seem quite at home, and they use the available props well. Against a 'beauty's recline' — the slanted bench of a pavilion — lounges a comely maiden while others sing prettily from a canopied boat. In the village square itself a bride arrives in a red sedan chair; the bridegroom's first glimpse of his bride was when her veil was lifted as she alighted from her sedan chair. In summer it is a relief to reach the rich man's house, which is powerfully (albeit anachronistically) air-conditioned and contains a number of interesting antiques. There is an excellent variety show — acrobats, dancers and a performance of martial arts. You can visit a fortune teller before repairing to the Restaurant of Plentiful Joy for a snack and some more music. The final exhibit is a large wax museum which includes a tableau of the boy Sung Emperor Ti Ching (see Museums) being carried on his uncle's back into the sea to drown, thus escaping capture by the invading Mongols.

The Sung Village is justly one of Hong Kong's most popular attractions. It has been well constructed with much attention to architectural detail — the project took five years and cost HK$15 million. The shop houses are more successful than the larger buildings, which look too new and glossy. It is necessary to join a tour (costing between HK$120–HK$155) except on Saturday and Sunday when the shows are not put on, and for HK$30 you can roam alone. There are four tours daily leaving by coach from six central points — your hotel will have details. Children love this tour.

When taking the dinner tour (which departs from the Furama Hotel at 4.20 pm and Lee Gardens Hotel at 4.30 pm), it is possible to combine a visit to the adjacent **Lai Chi Kok Amusement Park**. But you will have to take a taxi or bus back to your hotel. Although it is a conventional fun fair with ferris wheels, candyfloss and so on, Chinese Opera is performed here every evening from 7 pm to 7.30 pm. Another site well worth visiting in this area is the **Lei Cheung Uk Tomb and Museum** (see Museums).

The most practical method of visiting these attractions is by tour bus. But for a spot of adventure and a more direct experience of Hong Kong, why not forsake this comfortable-yet-sterile mode of transport and make an expedition to some of the rest of Kowloon's most interesting sights by MTR and on foot? Take the MTR — an experience in itself — to Wong Tai Sin Station, and follow the signs to the temple right beside it. This traditionally designed, large new temple, opened in 1973, is a *miu*, in other words dedicated to several creeds — Taoist, Buddhist and Confucian in this case. It is one of Hong Kong's most popular temples, and the crowds thronging it generate a sense of excitement. The site is in the midst of a concrete jungle of flats and is overlooked by the majestic Lion Rock which gives it excellent *fung shui*. (*Fung shui* — literally meaning wind and water — is said to influence the pattern of people's lives both for good and evil. To achieve the best *fung shui*, whether for a religious or secular building, the site is chosen by a professional geomancer and must combine harmony of the elements and the celestial world.) Enter the temple through its main gate, paying the ten cents entrance fee which goes to charity, pass Lord Buddha's delightful small pagoda and continue up to the terraces. Here the air buzzes with the shaking of *chim*, bamboo cylinders containing thin bamboo sticks, which are shaken until a stick drops out. The number on the stick corresponds to a message which is then bought from and interpreted by a soothsayer.

Unlike those of most temples, the inner sanctum is cordoned off, and entry is left to the discretion of the gatekeeper. The inside is very ornate, and in the centre of a huge gilt altar stands a portrait of the Taoist god Wong Tai Sin, who is thought to possess the power to heal. Many believers say that the water at his temple — although it comes straight from the public mains supply — has medicinal qualities. Down one side of the temple runs an alley full of soothsayers' stalls, decorated with all manner of charts and gaudy red Chinese calligraphy advising would-be customers of their talents.

The next stop on this expedition is the **Yaumatei Typhoon Shelter**. Take the MTR back to Yaumatei Station, emerge at the Portland Street exit and then walk east three blocks. As you approach the last block on the left, you will hear a strange clack-clack noise coming from an old building where there is a wholesale fruit market. Salesmen tout for business by clacking their mini abacuses like castanets.

Across the road is the Yaumatei Typhoon Shelter. It was built in 1915 after a disastrous typhoon and today is home to hundreds of families. These boat people are made up of two groups, the Tanka and Hoklo. The Tanka (immortalised in many works by Chinnery) are said to be the indigenous fisher folk of the South China Sea, while the Hoklo came later, possibly from Fukien province. They speak different dialects and can also be told apart by their junks and distinctive headgear (the Hoklo's reminiscent of Spanish style with a large horizontal brim, the Tanka's resembling a solar topee). The Tanka fish the deep waters and have larger vessels, whereas the Hoklo stick nearer to shore with their low-gunwaled, high sterned craft.

Historically, the boat people have suffered badly from discrimination. The Canton authorities used to refuse them the right to settle onshore, marry non-boat people or sit for civil service examinations, thereby excluding them from official positions. In Hong Kong, they were barred from living onshore until 1911, but today these communities are shrinking as many of their young people, no longer victims of discrimination, prefer to live on land. It is still fascinating to walk along the shelter: the community is almost self-sufficient with its shop sampans, barbers, school, doctors and so on. Some of the older junks are magnificent and serve not only as the homes of several generations but also of their dogs, chickens and invariably a Tin Hau shrine (see Festivals) wherein a light continuously burns.

One block beyond the south end of the shelter is Man Cheong Street, where a delicious smell of baking will make even the most disciplined nose twitch. Half-way along this street of bakeries is Heyton which makes mouth-watering Chinese custard tarts and other delights for the peckish adventurer. After indulging in these refreshments, cross Ferry Street, go along Kansu Street, and there, between 10 am and 4 pm at the intersection with Battery Street, you will find the **Jade Market**.

The pavement is covered with travelling salesmen's suitcases displaying all sorts of jade objects — predominantly bangles and pendants. Some lay their wares on gleaming white satin while others make do with crumpled newspaper. The more serious salesmen produce theirs in blue cloth boxes with white toggles. People are everywhere, browsing, haggling, and every now and then a small group gathers to examine a special piece. Serious sales are conducted silently with the aid of sign language, tic-tack style. (In Ch'ing times (1644–1911) interested parties would slip their hands inside each other's ample silk sleeves indicating their price by finger pressure.)

The Chinese regard for jade is perhaps best expressed by Confucius: 'It is soft, smooth and shining like kindness; it is hard, fine and strong, like intelligence; its edges seem sharp, but do not cut, like justice; it hangs down to the ground like humility; when struck, it gives a clear, ringing sound, like music; the stains in it which are not hidden and add to its beauty are like truthfulness; its brightness is like heaven, while its firm substance, born of mountains and the water, is like the earth'. In religious and domestic life jade has played an important role as the early Chinese believed it held the elixir of life. During the Han Dynasty (206 BC–AD 220) the wealthy were buried in suits of jade. Some of the greatest treasures of the Ming and Ch'ing Dynasties (1368–1911) are of finely worked jade. Today many people, even small children, wear a piece of jade as a talisman. It is said to be difficult to pick up a true bargain at the jade market but you never know your luck.

At the intersection of Canton Road and Jordan Road is **King George V Memorial Park**. Early in the morning this is crowded with people practising *tai chi ch'uan*. When performed by an expert, these balletic movements are a pleasure to watch, the idea being not only to exercise the body but also to achieve harmony of body and mind. It is worth looking in the park even later in the day as you may still find a late riser exercising.

Walk along Jordan Road eastwards and turn right up Shanghai Street into a bustling market area: slippery mounds of sea cucumbers — thought by some to be a delicacy — in pink buckets, neat squares of beancurd on thick wooden slabs, herbalist stalls, medicine shops emitting a strange yet nostril-cleansing smell, all interesting to see. Turn left into Bowring Street and find shop Number 36. This is filled from floor to ceiling with little bamboo cages holding birds of all sizes and colours, and even some crickets and squirrels. Outside the shop

you may see a huge pile of small brown paper parcels. When
unpacked, more bamboo cages are revealed, complete with charming
blue and white porcelain food and water bowls.

If you are able to resist the temptation of stopping for a delicious
dim sum lunch at Evergreen Restaurant, 136 Woosung Street, or one
of the many other restaurants in this small area, continue on eastwards
along Bowring Street into Nathan Road and the Jordan MTR Station
for your return to the modern world. At a gentle pace this meander
around Kowloon will take you about four hours.

There are a few other sites in this part of Kowloon that ought not
to missed and are worth making another expedition to the area to see.
For **Public Square Street** take the southernmost exit from the
Yaumatei MTR Station and walk two blocks south. Here you will find
a temple complex, fortune tellers and public letter writers —
surprisingly, a number of middle-aged Chinese are illiterate though this
situation is improving. Nearby in **Temple Street** Kun Wo Tung sells his
famed turtle meat soup — a medicinal cure-all. At dusk this street,
which in the old days was a favourite haunt of prostitutes, turns into a
colourful night market. For the **Bird Market** take the MTR to Mong
Kok Station, go two blocks west and then left into Hong Lok Street.
The birds in this truly fascinating spot are probably more pampered
than any other pets. Nearby is Wan Loi Restaurant, 484 Shanghai
Street, a tea house especially furnished to accommodate the bird lover
and his charge.

New Territories

Technically the area known as the New Territories includes all of Hong Kong except Kowloon, Stonecutter's Island and Hong Kong Island, but this section will deal only with the 281-square-mile land mass which sprawls between the Chinese border and the Kowloon Peninsula. The New Territories acquired their name on 11 June 1898 when Britain signed a 99-year lease with the Chinese on the pretext of providing a line of defence for Hong Kong Island and Kowloon. As part of the same concession Britain secured sole trading rights up the Yangtse River, thus protecting vital commercial interests from the ambitious French and Russians. Soon after this acquisition 'tales of its beauty and enchantment,' wrote a British historian, 'were passed back across the Kowloon hills — tales of paved mountain paths, walled villages of the plain . . . silent bays and silver sand.' Much of this unspoilt magic can still be found, but today it co-exists with dense urbanisation. Indeed the New Territories are undergoing one of the world's biggest urban development programmes. During the 1980s up to one-third of Hong Kong's total population will be rehoused in a series of vast new towns — some with populations of more than 500,000.

The duality of New Territories towns is exemplified by **Shatin**, once a small seaside town of 40,000 inhabitants. It is said that the rice grown here was so succulent that it was sent north to the emperor's table. But today its harbour has been filled in by literally bulldozing a hilltop into the water, and along with the surrounding fertile valley it has been transformed into a jungle of skyscrapers. But don't let this put you off; side by side with its concrete and steel Shatin offers plenty of cultural interest. Spectacularly sited in a bowl of jagged hills, it is an exciting first stop for a tour around the New Territories.

Shatin lies beyond the mountain range that protects Kowloon from the north. To get there by road drive through the **Lion Rock Tunnel**. You emerge below the **Amah Rock** (or Waiting-for-Husband Rock), shaped like a mother carrying her child. One legend is that her husband, a bodyguard at the Sung court in Kowloon (See Kowloon), was killed after a battle against the Mongols. Every evening she would climb this hill and vainly await his return, until eventually the gods took pity, released her soul and turned her body into stone. The rock can best be seen further down the Shatin Valley against the southern skyline where it is prominent.

Just before you reach Shatin is a living memento of the past, the well-preserved walled village named **Tsang Tai Uk**. High up on the tree-clad hill, **Tao Fong Shan**, overlooking Shatin from the northwest, is the **Chinese Mission to Buddhists** (strange as it may seem, it is a Lutheran organisation). In 1929 Karl Ludwig Reichelt, who had spent many years in China teaching Christianity to Buddhists, arrived in Hong Kong in search of a perfect site for a centre to study Buddhist literature. An expert in Chinese Buddhist architecture was employed, and in 1931 the foundations were laid for a delightful complex of buildings. An archway leads to the collection of blue-roofed whitewashed houses. The central building is a striking hexagonal chapel. A new guesthouse to accommodate 44 people has just been finished. There is a pottery decoration shop where the work is carried out by former Buddhist monks; the motifs are mostly floral or religious, but special orders are accepted. Throughout the compound are lovely plants and flowers, and the view of Shatin Valley is spectacular. There is no better place to spend two calm days if you can spare the time.

On the next hill stands the **Ten Thousand Buddha Monastery** with its hexagonal pink pagoda. It is reached by a stiff 500-step climb through a pine and bamboo wood — pretty except for the empty cans thrown everywhere. Round the walls of the main temple (built in 1950) are some 12,800 Buddhas of varying size. In front of the temple is the pink pagoda and to the right — a bizarre touch — a collection of children's fairground cars. If your tastes tend towards the macabre climb a little further up to the three temples above. Here you can see the embalmed body of the monastery's founder, the Reverend Yuet Kai. He died in 1965 aged 87, and, according to his wishes, was buried in a sitting position. Eight months later the body was exhumed and was said to be in perfect condition. It was then covered in gold leaf, and this diminutive figure now sits in a glass case on the altar. The wisps of hair protruding through the gold on the chin are said to be still growing.

While in Shatin it is impossible to miss the imposing **Shatin Racecourse**. Opened in 1978, the 250 acres of reclaimed land accommodate three tracks, stands for 37,000 race-goers, a central public park and a multitude of other buildings. Next door is the site of the impressive **Jubilee Sports Centre**.

Shatin boasts several delicious restaurants: **Luk Yuen** and **Lung Wah Hotel**, which specialise in pigeon, and the **New Shatin**, famous for stuffed nightshade flowers. But for a real surprise, go down a small steep track to the left of the main road descending from the Lion Rock Tunnel to the **Shatin Seafood Restaurant**. In addition to a menu of marine delicacies this obscure restaurant has one of the most distinguished wine lists (notably the first growth clarets) in Asia.

Continuing north from Shatin on the old Taipo Road you see the

Chinese University — an imposing 1960s acropolis commanding views both over the Shatin Valley and the serene lengths of the Tolo Harbour to the east. The University has some 4,500 students. Unlike the older Hong Kong University, the language of tuition is Chinese. Its museum is well worth a visit.

A little further on towards Taipo, built at the end of an isthmus, is **Island House**. During the Occupation it was used as the headquarters of the Japanese Commander of the New Territories. Stop on the road and contemplate a breathtaking view down Tolo Harbour — sparkling water, the occasional junk, mountains receding in layers, so characteristic of Chinese landscape.

Before going down into Taipo itself, turn off to **Taipo Kau**. Here there is a delightful rural English-style railway station and a ferry pier. Twice a day ferries leave for Tap Mun Island at the mouth of Tolo Harbour. The four-hour round trip, with stops at several islands and villages, affords an excellent glimpse of rural life. There are many permutations of this journey: the HKTA will give you all the timetables and advice needed. One can also get a ferry here for Ping Chau in Mirs Bay — not to be confused with Peng Chau, near Lantau — which is practically in Chinese territorial waters.

As early as the eighth century **Tolo Harbour** was known to have been a centre of the pearl fishing industry — in those days an extremely dangerous affair. The divers (who were Tanka people) were conscripted by the imperial household. They frequently had to be supervised by military guards to ensure that they worked and to prevent smuggling. The fishing system is described in a Yuan Dynasty petition which brought about its abolition on humanitarian grounds: 'The method of gathering them is to tie stones onto a man and lower him into the sea so he will sink quickly. Sometimes he gets pearls and sometimes not. When he suffocates he pulls the rope and a man in the boat hauls it up. If this is done a fraction too late.the man dies.'

Taipo itself, once a sleepy market town, is like Shatin, undergoing a metamorphosis. A hundred and twenty acres have been reclaimed from its seashore to build an industrial estate alongside the remains of the old market town (the market itself still operates nine times each lunar month). In June, Taipo is one of the favourite venues for the Dragon Boat Festival. On the road to Plover Cove Reservoir is a 280-year-old temple dedicated to Tin Hau, goddess of the sea.

Along the street is the marble-faced factory of the **Tai Ping Carpet Company**. Established in 1956, it is particularly proud of its list of 'prestigious installations', such as those in Buckingham Palace and the home of Bob Hope. On the floor below the plush showroom are the workshops. The workforce deftly injects row upon row of huge

hanging canvases with wool from a gun-like machine. Several types of pile and non-pile carpets are produced in both traditional and modern designs. To make an appointment to see the workshop telephone 0-6565161.

Continue along the north side of Tolo Harbour to the **Plover Cove Reservoir**; the next few miles over the watershed and down into Starling Inlet feature some of the most beautiful scenery accessible by road in the New Territories. **Brides Pool**, a little way off the road and along a stream, is a perfect picnic spot. In summer these hills are covered with flowers, wild gardenias, honeysuckle, rose myrtle; they are a flower and butterfly lover's dream.

Where the road joins Starling Inlet is the **Luk Keng Egretry**. From April to September this tree-clad hill is crowded with noisy egrets (small crane-like birds). Three species are indigenous to Hong Kong and all of their members, numbering about 800, nest here. These elegant birds can often be seen standing in a paddy, or sometimes on the back of water buffalo.

Farming is intensive between Luk Keng and Fanling mainly in the form of small, neat squares of vegetable gardens. The farming methods are still old-fashioned, with night soil often the only fertilizer used. The farmers are predominantly elderly, the young preferring easier factory work, and many of them are Hakka people. The Hakka women bending in the fields wear crownless straw hats with black cloth hanging from the brim — like a horse's tail it keeps the flies away when swished. The Hakka people have their own dialect and are one of the four groups of people in the New Territories, the others being the Punti, who speak Cantonese, and the two boat peoples (see Kowloon, page 000). For those interested in architecture, this area is rich in fine buildings including five walled villages (see the Government's excellent publication *Rural Architecture in Hong Kong*).

For a clear view of China go to Lok Ma Chau (Dismount Hill) border post. Legend has it that the last Sung emperor rested here, when fleeing from the Mongols, so those on the hill at the time had to dismount and kowtow in respect. The energetic can get an even clearer view by climbing up **Robin's Nest**.

Crossing over to the western side of the New Territories you reach **Kam Tin** where there are three walled villages all dating back some four or five centuries. Among the settlers who arrived during the late Sung Dynasty were the five Great Clans. The Tangs, who were the earliest to arrive, chose the most fertile land and became the most powerful. To protect themselves against bandits they surrounded their villages with sturdy walls which are still standing. **Kat Hing Wai** is the best known and is geared up for tourists with trinket-covered souvenir stalls. More interesting are **Wing Lung Wai** and **Shui Tau Tsuen**, particularly the latter's ancestral hall and Hung Shing Temple. In the aftermath of the 1949 Chinese Revolution, many thousands of refugees poured into the New Territories with little or no money to restart their farming activities. The philanthropic Kadoorie brothers realised the need for agricultural education and set up the Kadoorie Agricultural Aid Association. In the subsequent 30 years the project has snowballed: 1,218 villages have received help; 199 miles of road and 254 bridges have been constructed making formerly inaccessible areas available for cultivation; and through research and husbandry courses at the **Kadoorie Experimental Farm** (near Taipo), new farming methods have been accepted. It is possible to visit this 360-acre farm and garden (9.30 am−4.30 pm by appointment 0-981317). It has been beautifully landscaped, with exotic and native trees and plants blooming profusely.

Vast piles of empty oyster shells herald the fishing village of **Lau Fau Shan**. These oysters are either dried or made into oyster sauce rather than eaten raw. Situated on Deep Bay, the village is within a stone's throw of the mainland. Indeed it is across this stretch of water that many refugees attempt to swim. Seafood auctions are held every day in the main street, and the **Sun Tao Yuen Restaurant** provides all manner of seafood including, of course, oysters, which should only be eaten well-cooked. You can buy your own seafood and vegetables in the market and ask one of the restaurants to cook them up for you.

To the southwest of the New Territories are three interesting monasteries. **Castle Peak Monastery** is steeped in history. It stands high on Ching Shan (Green Mountain) overlooking Tuen Mun New Town and the long-since silted up Castle Peak Bay. This bay was the staging post for ships trading in and out of China — the pearls from Tolo Harbour were probably brought overland and shipped from here. *Tuen Mun* means 'garrisoned entrance', and the foundations of a fort believed to date from AD 750 have been found near the monastery. The monastery was founded, tradition says, by an eccentric Buddhist monk named *Pei Tu* (literally 'cup ferry' referring to the wooden bowl he carried around which he apparently used to cross water). A stone image of Pei Tu stands in a dark cove above the monastery where he used to meditate. A military commander is said to have put it here in his honour in AD 964. During the following centuries the monastery prospered, was rebuilt several times, and at one time was taken over for a short spell by the Taoists. Today it is inhabited by two Buddhist monks and three followers. The delightful complex of buildings includes a large, slightly tilted, restaurant which serves vegetarian meals. This leads onto a spacious terrace backed with 'evening

Mai Po

by Clive Viney
— co-author, *Birds of Hong Kong*

Many international flights approach Hong Kong by following the Pearl River to its mouth on the South China Sea. From the air and for most part, this is an endless waterscape of small ponds along the banks of the mighty river until, as the plane begins its descent, the scars of China's great economic experiment at Shen Zhen are clearly visible. Then, amidst the greys, blues and browns, a patch of vivid green stands out like an emerald — Mai Po.

The green is the great, thick belt of mangroves on the eastern shore of Deep Bay. They survive only because Mai Po is a nature reserve. Elsewhere around the bay, the mangroves originally were cropped for fuel but in recent years have been cleared for reclamation, river training, rubbish and ash lagoons and even airport feasibility studies. This is a sad loss, for precious little mangrove remains anywhere on the China coast. It is not just the unique community of salt tolerant plants and animals that is lost but also an essential nursery for prawn and fish stocks.

Mai Po sits almost in a no-man's land between Hong Kong and China, but administratively it is part of the New Territories. Behind the mangrove belt, the reserve comprises a collection of large and very long ponds. Most of these ponds are tidal with water levels artifically controlled for prawn and, to a lesser degree, fish farming. However, the Hong Kong chapter of the World Wide Fund for Nature has secured the control of several of these ponds and manages them especially to attract wildlife. For instance, when the tide is high in Deep Bay, covering the vast mudflats, mud is available, in the safety of the reserve, for the hundreds, and sometimes thousands, of feeding and roosting birds. For the visitor, viewing hides or blinds have been strategically placed to permit close observation, and a new education centre provides much background information and a useful bookshop.

Internationally, Deep Bay is vitally important as a stopping-off and feeding point for migratory birds. These are the birds that breed in the far north during the brief summer but spend the remainder of the year in warmer climes away to the south, even as far as Australia and New Zealand. Obviously, such long journeys, which are undertaken twice a year, cannot be made without safe resting places. And with the rapid development of China such staging posts have all but vanished. If the vast nutrient-rich mudflats of Deep Bay (a misnomer for its average depth is just three metres) were to disappear, either through reclamation or more insidiously through pollution, then these migratory birds would die. Entire species might vanish. Already a number of species that visit annually are close to extinction; these range from huge Dalmation Pelicans to the extraordinary Spoon-billed Sandpiper, but others include a gull so rare that its breeding grounds have only just been discovered and an egret that has all but vanished. Because the mud is treacherously soft, the bay is difficult to approach. Local fisherman use mud scooters, propelled by one foot, to tend their oysterbeds. Visitors to Mai Po can now reach the mud via an exciting floating broadwalk, which penetrates the mangroves, to a viewing hide which rises and falls with the tide. Perhaps Hong Kong's greatest wilderness experience is to sit in this outer hide and watch the rising tide creep over the mud, moving the great mass of feeding birds closer and closer until they are forced to rise up, as the last vestige of mud is covered, and seek sanctuary in the reserve.

In the context of Hong Kong, Mai Po is vital. No other place in this over-populated territory can boast such a wealth of wildlife. Well over 250 species of birds have been recorded and mammals include leopard cats, civet cats, crab-eating mongoose and even the occasional otter. It is quite unbelievable that only 45 minutes from Central or Tsimshatsui, by car, there is true wilderness. From the minute of arrival birds are evident everywhere. Overhead are herons, egrets, ibises and brilliant blue kingfishers; the bushes and reeds are full of warblers and white-eyes, and on the path ahead are invariably wagtails and buntings. It is not just the birds that make a trip to Mai Po worthwhile; venture forth into the mangroves and watch the antics of the calling fiddler crabs or the comical mudskippers, fish that live both in and out of water.

The Chinese government has also recognised the importance of the area and declared 11 kilometres of the Deep Bay shoreline, contiguous with Mai Po, a strict nature reserve. On the face of it, the future looks rosy. However, the hinterland is developing at an alarming rate and the fragile ecosystem of the mud itself is under constant threat from horrendous pollution.

Despite these worries, everybody involved with the Mai Po project is highly optimistic. It has become an oasis for wildlife amidst an urban desert. Every season more and more birds, in an ever-increasing variety, visit the reserve. Even at the height of summer, usually the quietest time, Mai Po is well worth a visit as, apart from sheltering the many breeding birds, the mangrove and shore communities are at their most active.

The Hong Kong chapter of the World Wildlife Fund organises daily guided tours. Individual visits are possible for bona fide naturalists but a permit must first be obtained from the Agriculture and Fisheries Department of the Hong Kong Government. The Hong Kong Bird Watching Society holds regular weekend field meetings and is always ready to welcome visiting birdwatchers. Soon, part of the reserve will be opened up to the public on a casual basis, and a captive wildfowl collection of Asian birds is to be established.

Mai Po is a little known face of Hong Kong that should not be missed.

fragrance' bushes, whose exquisite smell is not just confined to the evening. The stunning view was beautifully described by the Confucian scholar Han Yue (AD 820) who 'looked over the vast unfathomable ocean and the forests and water and felt that it was indeed a sacred spot'. Another of the monastery's treasures is the '10,000-year-old bone of a dragon' which is housed in a cage under an ancient gnarled tree literally balancing on its roots. If possible, visit this outstanding monastery with a Mandarin speaker. The abbot has a wealth of historic anecdotes.

Some early foundations from the Han Dynasty have also been found at **Lingtou Monastery**, though the present building with its seven altars is merely 200 years old. It is inhabited by one monk who has to cope with severe security problems arising from the monastery's isolated position. Indeed, although it is only 15 minutes from Castle Peak Monastery, many local people do not know of its existence, so go armed with precise instructions from the HKTA.

The Taoist monastery **Ching Chung Koon** (close to Castle Peak Hospital), although of traditional design, was founded in 1949. It includes an old people's home which is funded with the help of the monastery's popular vegetarian restaurant. It has an extensive library and some priceless works of art. For those interested in bonsai, there are marvellous examples everywhere.

Far away at the western entrance to Hong Kong is the fishing village of **Lei Yue Mun**, traditionally the haunt of pirates and until recently only accessible by boat (still the most exciting way of getting there; a pre-dinner trip through the harbour is particularly recommended). Today, it is the haunt of seafood lovers. The system of dining here requires a curious division of labour. Wander down the narrow streets edged with bubbling fish tanks and gaudy signs, bargain for the fish of your choice (a Cantonese-speaking friend will be invaluable here), then, armed with flapping plastic bags, choose a restaurant in which to have your purchases cooked and served. **Wai Lung Seafood Restaurant** is popular, always jostling with people both eating and playing mahjong. Finish off a delicious meal by stopping at a stall making fresh, paper-thin egg rolls. A blob of batter is dropped onto a sizzling pan and then deftly rolled up. The stall next to Number 41B on the playground corner is to be recommended.

A separate limb of the New Territories land mass is the extravagantly beautiful and mountainous **Saikung Peninsula** which contains lovely parkland for hiking and swimming. Sai Kung town, half new, half old, has a typically cluttered Chinese market. Along the waterfront are several restaurants, their outside tables decked with bright tablecloths. The brave can take their fish to the Sam Hoi (Three

River) Restaurant, which is built on stilts over the sea and serves delicious noodles. Before leaving visit the attractive Tin Hau temple.

Many traditional beliefs are still adhered to in these rural areas. In Long Keng near Sai Kung an ancient banyan tree is worshipped. Trees reputedly house the soul of a god who can prevent sickness and aid fertility. A shrine is often placed on or at the foot of the tree and, to ward off evil spirits, strips of red paper decorate it. Another important village deity is the Well God, who keeps the village water supply both topped up and pure. His shrine will often be found beside a well.

One of the most picturesque features of the Saikung Peninsula is **Rocky Harbour**, an enormous island-strewn stretch of water carved out of its southeast flank. A trip undertaken by few visitors but well worthwhile is an exploration of Rocky Harbour by boat, hiring a small craft from Hebe Haven pier (the HKTA will suggest whom to contact). This opens up endless possibilities to visit sandy coves, small islands and remote villages.

Outlying Islands

Lantau

The Hong Kong archipelago consists of 235 islands. Some of these barely qualify as they comprise just a few rocks. However, the largest, Lantau, is twice the size of Hong Kong Island. This is a staggeringly beautiful world of mountains, mists, monasteries — it is sometimes called the Island of Prayer — peace and calm. With its predominantly mountainous terrain and little industrial development, Lantau supports a population of only some 20,000. Try and visit during the week: it becomes crowded with day trippers and campers at the weekends.

Although knowledge of Lantau's early history is sparse, it is believed to have been settled since prehistoric times. In 1277 the doomed last emperor of the Sung Dynasty fled to Lantau from the New Territories. Some say a temporary court was set up in the Tung Chung valley — indeed several families claim to be direct descendants of the Sung courtiers. Recently constructed **Discovery Bay** is a commercial/residential resort, with a commuter as well as weekend population. Discovery Bay Golf Club and Village Resort are open to the public with a wide range of recreational facilities, including an 18-hole golf course, tennis courts, swimming pool, water sports and billiards. Discovery Bay has its own high-speed ferry service which runs from Blake Pier in Central.

Ferries run from the Outlying Districts Pier in Central to **Silvermine Bay** (about one hour) on the east coast or Tai O on the far west coast. From Silvermine Bay you can hire a car or take a bus across the island and then return on the ferry from Tai O. Some of the Silvermine Bay ferries stop at Peng Chau. (Do not disembark unless you wish to visit Lantau's **Trappist Monastery** dedicated to Our Lady of Joy. The monks' boat meets every Peng Chau ferry and for about HK$2 will take you across the small channel to the foot of a flight of steps leading to the monastery. Each day the monastery's cows produce 1,000 pints of milk and its chickens 600–700 eggs. You can walk from here to Silvermine Bay in about two hours.)

At Silvermine Bay the bus terminal and taxi stand are just opposite the ferry exit. To hire a minibus or car with driver, telephone Lantau Tours at 5-9848256 before leaving Hong Kong Island. There is little to see in Silvermine Bay itself (silver was mined there only briefly during the last century). Along the beach are a group of good seafood restaurants: the Sampan (formerly Ned Kelly's Last Stand) and Seaview also serve Western food. **Pui O** nestling under the majestic Sunset Peak is the next village on the road. It has a selection of guesthouses and restaurants and across some meadows is a long, slightly grey beach. Lantau's most beautiful beach accessible by road is at **Cheung Sha**, between Pui O and the Shek Pik Reservoir.

For the walker, Lantau is a paradise, but it is easy to get lost (or worse) on its precipitous terrain. Wear snake proof shoes, take a strong stick, a good map and sensible precautions. *Selected Walks in Hong Kong* and the HKTA's leaflet *Lantau Walks* are useful companions. For a beautiful walk that is neither particularly hazardous nor too taxing, turn left down Wang Pui Road just after the Shek Pik Reservoir (if you are in a car you will have to leave it by the waterworks barrier) and take the path along the headland to **Fan Lau** (about three hours) where there is a ruined fort and two small isolated beaches. From Fan Lau it is possible to hire a junk or if you feel energetic to walk the five miles round to Tai O to catch the homeward ferry.

Continuing on from Shek Pik Reservoir the road winds up between dense vegetation and then at the watershed opens out to display a beautiful valley with the Pearl Estuary beyond it. The hillside on the right is dominated by two monastery buildings, Po Lin and Yin Hing, their yellow roofs shining against the dark green vegetation. No fewer than 135 monasteries dot Lantau, the most famous and largest being **Po Lin Monastery** (Temple of Precious Lotus). It is situated 2,500 feet above sea level and was first used by monks in 1905 but not inaugurated as a monastery until 1927. Its present buildings date from 1970. There are 100 resident monks and nuns who, with the help of about a hundred retired people, look after the monastery and manage a commercial tourist enterprise. Their vegetarian restaurant brings in roughly HK$50,000 per month. Two thousand tourists visit the community most weekends but it is planned to increase this by building a cable car up from the valley. On stepping out of the cable car the visitor will then see a 30-foot standing Buddha. The ornate main temple is dedicated to the Three Precious Buddhas and the stone floor is inlaid with the lotus pattern. To Buddhists the lotus is the symbol of the attainability of *nirvana* whatever one's past: 'It grows out of mud but it is not defiled'. You can reach the monastery by bus or on foot, spend the night there, then climb neighbouring **Lantau Peak** (3,000 feet above sea level), and watch the sunrise.

A ten-minute walk from the monastery, on **Ngong Ping Plateau**, is a tea plantation. In 1959 a British barrister, with experience in Ceylon, noticed some disused tea terraces in the area. Today, there is a 70-acre farm producing 36,000 pounds of tea (both Indian and Chinese) per annum.

The road to the small town of **Tai O** is bordered by the dry fields of old salt pans. Two hundred years ago Tai O salt factories flourished,

and today Tai O remains a large producer of salt fish. The village is built half on Lantau, half on another island, and is connected by a charming flat-bottomed ferry pulled and poled by two old ladies (fare 50 cents). At the far end of the village on the island side stands **Hou Wang Temple**, which was built in 1699 (reigned over by the Ch'ing Emperor K'ang Hsi) and dedicated to Marquis Yang Liang Chieh, the uncle and guardian of the last Sung Emperor. Each year a festival is held in his memory: an enormous theatre is constructed in the temple's forecourt, and opera is performed. The houses along the shore are curious looking, to say the least, being constructed of upturned boats incarcerated in metal sheeting. This method is used to contrive even two-storeyed affairs, complete with verandahs and roof gardens. Often the house fronts are supported picturesquely on stilts in the water. Nearly every second shop in the village sells its famed salt fish which hang like Italian salamis, their heads neatly packaged in paper. Tai O has some other lovely old shops, including an 80-year-old traditional medicine shop (some way down along Wing On Street on the Lantau side), where sandalwood and herbs perfume the air.

The only road to **Tung Chung** on the northern shore climbs over the central spine of Lantau, overlooked from their hillside vantage point by several monasteries, and with Sunset Peak towering to the right. The remains of a 17th-century fort stand guard over Tung Chung; its six cannons have been recently restored.

Cheung Chau

Lantau's small neighbour Cheung Chau has a thriving fishing community. For hundreds of years this island was the haunt of pirates, traders and smugglers; today, and with an area of one square mile, it almost has double the population of Lantau. Its main street buzzes with the activity of a typical market with plenty of food and drinks stalls for the hot and footsore visitor. Try the seafood at the floating restaurant, **Cheung Chau Marriage Boat**. After wandering in the market and its side streets — there are several good jade shops where occasionally bargains can be found — visit the **Pak Tai Temple** (to the left when you get off the ferry). This is the setting for the famed Cheung Chau Bun Festival (see Festivals). The temple, built in 1783, houses an early statue of Pak Tai — the god of the north — and a Sung Dynasty sword salvaged from the sea during the last century.

By crossing the thin central strip of land it is possible to make a circular walk around the southern part of the island. The beaches along Peak Road (named somewhat obscurely **Tun Wan**, **Afternoon**, **Morning** and **Italian**) are all good for a cooling swim. Just beyond the

Italian beach is the Cheung Po Tsai hideout cave. From Sai Wan Village, either walk or take a sampan back to the ferry pier.

Peng Chau

Peng Chau is a much quieter place. Although its 8,000 inhabitants are predominantly fisherfolk, there is some cottage industry, including several porcelain factories. Yuet Tong have a factory employing 100 people. Like Cheung Chau the island has no motor cars and you can wander peacefully through the narrow streets. There are noodle stalls and restaurants aplenty. You can buy your fish on the pier and take it to **Sun Kwong Restaurant** (tel. 5-9830239) to be cooked. On the way to the porcelain factories, depending on the weather, you may see tray upon tray of tiny fish drying in the sun.

Lamma

Just south of Aberdeen lies Lamma, at five square miles Hong Kong's third largest island. Fragments unearthed in Shan Wan Bay, and stone rings attributed to the Shan Yao aboriginal people, provide evidence of Lamma's prehistoric background. Today this rugged mountainous island of sparse vegetation has a population of 5,000 people engaged in vegetable and fish farming and some cottage industry. It has lovely beaches but unfortunately the water is often polluted.

There are two main villages on Lamma, both served by ferries leaving from Hong Kong's Outlying Districts Pier. Alternatively you can take your life in your hands, hire a sampan from Aberdeen and make a dash across the paths of giant container ships into **Sok Kwu Wan**. There is little to see in the village but plenty to eat, as a whole series of outdoor restaurants lines the shore. North of here St George's Bay, with its small Tin Hau temple and fishing community, is the scene once a year of spectacular Dragon Boat Races (see Festivals). To enable more crews to compete, these races are held on a separate day to the gazetted festival day. Here the traditional religious part of the festival is observed punctiliously, every team bringing its lion dancers and offerings to pay homage to Tin Hau at the temple. If you are visiting Hong Kong in early June, do not miss it.

From Sok Kwu Wan it is a gentle two-hour walk, mostly along the coast, passing desirable (depending on the tides) **Hung Shing Ye beach** and Hong Kong's enormous new power station. You end up at **Yung Shue Wan**, where you can catch a ferry back to Central. This small town also has a number of seafood restaurants.

Other Islands

The two ferries that call each day at Sok Kwu Wan continue on to **Po Toi**, a group of four rocky islands. The largest, Po Toi, has a delightful small village of brightly painted houses, which are slightly Mediterranean in feeling and built around a wide bay. This bay is the scene of a colourful rural festival on the birthday of goddess Tin Hau in May (see Festivals, page 80). By clambering round the rocks from the village you will come upon some rock carvings, allegedly 3,500 years old, which are thought to have been made by Burmese or Khmer people. After the exhausting scramble back, visit the restaurant on the right (looking from the sea) serving ice-cold beer and delicious fish.

In addition to these more accessible islands the group in **Rocky Harbour** (see New Territories, page 141) is highly recommended for a visit. **Double Haven** is really too remote to be discovered by any but the luckiest or most pioneering of short-term visitors. This is a natural harbour formed by a group of islands in Mirs Bay very close to the Chinese mainland. Quite simply it offers some of the most beautiful sea and mountainscapes in the world.

Tours in Hong Kong

Local entrepreneurial talents have produced an astonishingly wide selection of tours in Hong Kong. Enthusiastic brochures encourage you to sip cocktails while travelling on a tram from Causeway Bay to Western, or go on shopping expeditions with American expatriate wives, or drive up the Peak for a 'night view' and down again to Wanchai to sample a 'night spot.'

All these things (without the frills) can of course be done alone. But if you do opt for a tour, then select with caution or you may find yourself simply on a glorified shopping expedition to spots where your guide is assured a percentage. And be aware that touring by coach, especially in the New Territories, may turn out to be half a day of sitting in heavy traffic staring at unsightly, half-constructed new towns.

Probably most worthwhile is Hong Kong Watertours, which has an impressive range of trips of different lengths, some combining sea and land touring, others simply offering relaxed drinks or meals on board while the boat sails past parts of Hong Kong's varied shoreline — more comfortable, more isolated and much more expensive than just taking the usual public ferry. Two other interesting and well organised tours are a visit to the Sung Dynasty Village (see Kowloon, page 131) and a cruise on the Hong Kong Hilton's *Wan Fu* — a replica of a 19th-century Royal Navy pirate chaser. Make bookings at your hotel.

Excursions from Hong Kong

Tours to China

The great majority of those crossing the border into neighbouring Guangdong Province are Hong Kong Chinese visiting relatives, but the Territory increasingly acts as the main gateway into China for foreigners. Thousands of tourists and businessmen begin their China travels in Hong Kong on a train, plane or hovercraft bound for Guangzhou (Canton).

China Travel Service (HK) Limited (CTS) is the agent in Hong Kong for China International Travel Service which handles all aspects of foreign travel within China. CTS offers a range of group tours lasting from three to 14 days to several different parts of China. It also offers more pricey 'individual tours' to a number of cities which is a little more flexible than the usual group tour. The most attractive longer tours tend to get booked up well in advance, but the last-minute traveller may be able to get on them if there are cancellations. CTS offices are at 77 Queen's Road Central (tel. 5-220450) and 27–33 Nathan Road (tel. 3-667201). Most travel agents in Hong Kong will handle the booking of CTS tours to China (for which they receive a flat commission).

An increasing number of Hong Kong's tour operators and agents are running their own tours, bypassing CTS and negotiating directly with the authorities in China. Some of these tours may be more expensive, but they may also offer extra facilities which a straight CTS tour does not (an escort from the Hong Kong office, for example, to iron out all problems that inevitably greet travellers in China). It is worth checking carefully on these points before selecting your tour. Competition is of course keen in Hong Kong, especially among operators and agents offering short trips (six days in Peking, three in Canton, four or five in Shanghai, for example) and cheaper tour prices may simply indicate that agents are undercutting each other.

Day trips to China

CTS offer two tours from Hong Kong — one just over the border to Shenzhen (spelt Shumchun in Hong Kong) and the other to the county of Zhongshan (Chungshan) entering China through Macau. Of the two, the trip via Macau is by far the superior. It takes you by hydrofoil from Hong Kong to Macau (70 minutes) where you cross the border into an attractive landscape of ricefields and traditional Cantonese villages. A tour bus takes you to the birthplace of Dr Sun Yat-Sen (regarded by the Chinese as the founder of modern China) and on to a county town for lunch. On the way back to Macau you visit a commune, fishing village or kindergarten. The cheaper trip to Shenzhen offers less chance to see anything of Guangdong Province. The town, with 300,000 or so inhabitants, is distinctly untypical since it is the hub of one of China's Special Economic Zones, established to attract foreign (particularly Hong Kong) investment and technology. High-rise residential and commercial blocks are under construction, industry is growing, and accompanying social problems associated with the town's sudden economic boom are much in evidence. A visit to the Shenzhen Reservoir, which is one of the main suppliers of water to Hong Kong, is included in this visit.

Day trips to Macau

Macau

The Portuguese enclave of Macau lies only 60 kilometres (37.3 miles) away from Hong Kong, but it is surprising what a different world awaits you at the end of the one-hour jetfoil journey. Stroll five minutes from the pier and you step back four centuries, into a world of cobbled streets, venerable banyans, and churches founded soon after the Portuguese arrived in 1557.

It is safe to say that no other place in the world can match Macau's blend of architectural traditions, mostly harmonious, sometimes incongruous, but always interesting. Sino-Iberian is the basic style, with overlays, underlays and sometimes highlights from a dozen traditions incorporated in a single pediment or balcony. Dutch, Moorish, Spanish, Japanese and Italian traders, and residents all made distinctive contributions to this six-mile square melting pot of cultures. Very little remains from the earliest days: most of the sumptuous churches were rebuilt in the last century; the Leal Senado, with its magnificent wood-panelled library and council room, dates back little more than 100 years. Art Deco and Art Nouveau were strong influences in the 1920s when Macau had its first building boom. Looking at some of the charming survivors of this era, it is intriguing to spot where other influences came into play.

In Macau the pace of everything is slower than in nearby Hong Kong, but in recent years development has been proceeding quickly, as you can see and hear in many parts of the city. Nevertheless, residents have a keen sense of the value of their past and a feeling for conservation has strengthened in recent years. New paint has brought about a blossoming of geranium pink and red, fresh peppermint green, ochre and umber in many formerly dilapidated areas. A limited

amount of more ambitious restoration work has been carried out on several prominent government buildings.

The spruced up buildings are by no means empty shells: they form part of Macau's day-to-day fabric. Some serve as government or commercial offices, others are private residences or shops, and a few have been given renewed purpose as museums. As you walk around Macau (and this is definitely a place to explore on foot) glance upwards. Above the street-level plate glass and fluorescent lights of many a hairdressing salon, electrician, cake shop, bank and boutique sit capiz shell window panes, or delightful fancies from the mid-19th century.

This is an easy place to explore at your own pace with the help of some of the excellent leaflets and maps obtainable free from the Macau Department of Tourism. The leaflet called *Walking Tours* is particularly good. You can also pick up most of this material at the Macau Tourist Information Bureau in Hong Kong — Room 305, on the third floor of the Shun Tak Centre where you board your vessel for Macau. You can reserve hotel accommodation and tours here, too. Try to avoid the weekends or public holidays when you plan a trip to Macau. And it is always a good idea to buy your return ticket before leaving Hong Kong: you can always join the stand-by queue to travel back earlier if you wish, and you can change to a later sailing provided you do this well ahead of your scheduled departure time. Tickets can be bought at Ticketmate outlets in many places in Hong Kong or in the Shun Tak Centre.

If you are tired or visiting widely separated destinations, taxis are usually easy to find and fares are low. Carry a map to help when dealing with the majority of drivers who do not understand English. Macau also has pedicabs for short distances. Don't miss the facade of St Paul's, Lin Fong Miu, Kun Iam Tong, Teatro Dom Pedro, Luis de Camoes Garden and Museum, Protestant Cemetery, Lou Lim Ioc Garden, St Joseph's Seminary and Leal Senado (go inside to see the raised garden, and the beautiful wood-panelled library). You cannot go far without stumbling upon an intriguing site in this melange of past and present.

Spare time for the two outlying islands, which are relatively unspoiled despite the density of population on peninsular Macau. Use the public buses, charter a taxi for a couple of hours or use an international driving licence to hire a Macau Moke (arrange this in Hong Kong or on the spot). It's easy to miss the tiny village behind the government buildings and temple off Taipa's main square. Explore the narrow alleyways, enjoy the warm Iberian colours of the diminutive houses and stumble on yet another section of the marvellous mosaic that is Macau.

After the museums, monuments and mementoes, complete your Macau experience with the unique flavours of Macanese food. Like everything else about Macau, the cooking has been formed by a host of influences from around the world, successfully combined with the Portuguese-Chinese base from which all its dishes have developed. African chicken, chilli crabs or garlic prawns are distinctive and delicious. So also are the rich stews and soups based on Portuguese country cuisine. And along with the olives, codfish and spicy chourizo sausage, no Macau meal is complete without its complement of Portuguese wines and a brandy to finish. Dine in style surrounded by sparkling crystal and gleaming silver at restaurants in Macau's leading hotels. Or opt for the more homely atmosphere of some of Macau's humbler establishments where chickens and puppies keep you company.

The majority of Macau's visitors are Hong Kong people in search of gambling. They head straight from the pier to the casinos, the canidrome or the trotting track, leaving the rest of Macau to the enterprising few. If you decide to make your Macau visit more than a day trip, it is worth bearing in mind that the enclave's hotels offer very good value, especially mid-week, when some attractive package deals are available at most seasons of the year.

The Mandarin Oriental provides five-star comfort and elegance, with service and facilities to match. Part of an internationally-renowned hotel group, it has a guest to staff ratio of 1:1. Outdoor swimming pools, sauna, exercise area, jacuzzi, massage, tennis courts and squash courts are all included in the health centre. There is a small 24-hour casino within the hotel.

The Hyatt Regency, located in idyllic surroundings on Taipa Island, is the ultimate in getting away from it all. Its Resort Centre caters to all tastes, providing everything from professional tennis coaching and aerobics classes to aromatherapy beauty treatments and poolside sunbathing loungers. **Alfonso's** prepares outstanding Portuguese and Macanese specialities.

Pousada de Sao Tiago must be one of the most romantic and luxurious hotels in the world, nestling inside the walls of a 16th-century fortress, in an unrivalled location overlooking the South China Sea. It has 23 rooms decorated in traditional Portuguese style — hand-carved mahogany furniture and individually-crafted Portuguese tiles and crystal chandeliers.

Hotel Bela Vista dates back to early Victorian days and it sometimes seems that little has changed in the meantime. Every few years ambitious renovations are announced, but for the moment it remains a favourite with savvy Hong Kong visitors, as much on

account of its intractably nostalgic atmosphere as its modest prices. Try for an upstairs sea-view balcony room. Or at least leave time for a leisurely coffee or glass of wine on the balcony of the restaurant, if not a more detailed exploration of the imaginative menu featuring Macanese dishes.

The Lisboa Hotel seems designed for compulsive gamblers who wish to spend as little time as possible away from the casinos within its confines. Despite the tawdry and noisy surroundings, its restaurants, **A Galera** and **Portas do Sol**, are elegant havens of gastronomic delight at surprisingly affordable prices.

Other restaurants providing excellent and distinctive food at the time of writing include **Gallo** in Taipa Village; **1999** in Coloane Park (adjacent to the walk-through aviary); **Fernando's Place** at *Hac Sa*, the black sand beach; **Henri's: Solmar**; **Pinocchio**; and **Portuguesa**.

Restaurants

An indication of costs is given below. One star means inexpensive (below HK$75 per person), two stars mean moderately expensive (HK$75–HK$175), three stars mean verging on the costly (HK$175–HK$250), and four stars represents HK$250 and over per head, all excluding alcoholic drinks. In the case of Chinese restaurants, prices are per person but calculated for parties of four to six.

Chinese

American Restaurant
**

20 Lockhart Road,
Wanchai, Hong
Kong,
tel. 5-277277

美利堅飯店
灣仔駱克道20號

Exactly the sort of name to push one on in search of somewhere less obviously touristy, but this excellent Peking restaurant does not just serve Peking duck but highly recommended winter dishes such as hotpots and mutton with bunches of spring onion, fried and steamed dumplings and, another winter favourite, delicious Tsientsin cabbage in chicken oil. Staff are helpful and will suggest seasonal dishes; what they cannot do is make more room for you during the very crowded lunch hours — so book ahead and when you get there, see what others have plumped for and order the same.

Fung Lum **
Siu Yat Lau,
Sai Kung, Kowloon,
tel. 3-7926623,
      3-7921346

楓林小館
西貢兆日樓
沙田材林45號

This is a Cantonese-style chain which extends from the New Territories to California but still preserves its high standards. Even those hitherto unsure of beancurd should find one of the almost 20 varieties to their taste, and the breadth of the menu is such that only the largest parties feel that they are not missing something special. The smoked duck they recommend reaches you after an intriguingly complicated preparation in which the bird is scalded, wind-dried, smoked over wood chips, tea and charcoal and then steamed. Also try the sliced beef with chilli and bean sauce. Shrimp baked with salt is more Hakka than Cantonese but tastes delicious — as does the chicken with lemon sauce (ask the waiter not to make it too sweet).

Incidentally, Fung Lum also manage the Yucca de Lac restaurant (tel. 0-6912011) on Lot 716 in Ma Liu Shiu village, overlooking the harbour on the Taipo Road above Shatin. It specializes in Cantonese-style seafood and has a beautiful view, which is why the Hong Kong Tourist Association chose it as a stop on their Land Between tour. Other Fung Lum locations include: 45 Tsuen Nam Road, Shatin, New Territories, tel. 0-6921175, 0-6911484.

Great Shanghai **
26 Prat Avenue,
1st Floor, Kowloon,
tel. 3-668158

大上海飯店
尖沙咀寶勒巷26號

There are some who consider this to be the best Shanghai restaurant anywhere in the city. Certainly the restaurant does not stint on peppers, oils or garlic, and their seafood is as good as any in Shanghai itself. But with Hong Kong's abundance of fresh ingredients, Great Shanghai has created an imaginative menu. Specials include chicken in wine sauce, shrimps, braised eels with bamboo shoots and noisette of pork served with vegetables and covered in a heavy soy sauce.

Jade Garden **
Swire House,
1st Floor, Central,
Hong Kong,
tel. 5-239966

翠園酒樓
中環太古大廈2樓

Almost a case of eating by numbers (as well as in numbers). No one has ever accused Jade Garden of introducing a note of excess excitement into the Hong Kong culinary experience, but then again few complain. You know where you stand with a Jade Garden menu, the staff are ready to point out the standard dishes and are almost as speedy in bringing them to your table. Their banquets include barbecued pork, mushrooms and vegetables and apple fritters, not forgetting, of course, the beggar's chicken.
    Jade Garden is part of the massive Maxim's group (who also own the ultra-acceptable and upmarket Guangzhou Garden, Exchange Square, tel. 5-251163) and is known for its reasonable prices and absolute reliability, which can prove a reassuring blessing, even in the gourmet paradise of

Hong Kong. Other Jade Garden locations include: 30 Queen's Road, Entertainment Building, Hong Kong, tel. 5-234071; 53 Paterson Street, Causeway Bay, Hong Kong, tel. 5-778282; 1 Hysan Avenue, Causeway Bay, Hong Kong, tel. 5-779332; Star House, 4th Floor, Tsimshatsui, Kowloon, tel. 3-7226888; BCC Building, Carnarvon Road, Tsimshatsui, Kowloon, tel. 3-698311; East Asia Garden, Texaco Road, Tsuen Wan, New Territories, tel. 0-4163681.

King Bun Restaurant ***
158 Queen's Road, Central, Hong Kong, tel. 5-434256, 5-432223

敬賓酒家
中環皇后大道中
158號

Doyen of Chinese food writers, Willie Mark, dubs King Bun the best Cantonese restaurant in the city, which is tribute indeed but easy to understand. The whole feel of the place is of serious expertise, and the menu is dauntingly large so that one keeps craning for clues from what others have ordered. This is the place to confirm what sweet and sour pork really should taste like, with green and red peppers and Chinese onion added in just the right balance. They also have excellent pigeon, Yunnanese ham casserole and barbecued duck. Come winter, try the braised bear's paw, deer and other game, and the incomparable snake soup. Warning: it is not a place to go on your own or without a Chinese friend, but in a large party, with a Cantonese speaker, you will enjoy a banquet to remember.

Luk Yu Restaurant **
24–26 Stanley Street, Central, Hong Kong, tel 5-235463/4/5

陸羽茶室
中環士丹利街
24-26號

'Old, revered, but brusque' is how one writer recently described this old, established (1925) restaurant which many regard as a temple to *yum cha* and the morning ritual of drinking tea with *dim sum*. Named after the god of tea, the restaurant has a marvellous old feel to it, with its lacquered chairs, marble tables, mirrored cupboards and brass spittoons. Its four storeys seat 500, but beware of rushing in because no English menus are available and the dishes are not paraded around for you to order by gesture. On the other hand, the waiters are helpful and will choose on your behalf such delicacies as meat dumplings cooked with tangerine peel, minced ham in thousand-layer cake, fried shrimp roll, roasted duck with rice in lily leaves and many more. Dinner is also served, but the menu makes no mention of the specials on offer so, again, you will be at the mercy of the staff. Try to avoid the busy morning time. Most locals agree it is best to go with a Chinese friend later in the day.

Lung Wah Hotel ** Lot 156, 22 Ha Wo Che, Shatin, New Territories, tel. 0-6911594

龍華酒店 新界沙田下禾輋22號

This is an astonishing restaurant if you love pigeon. Several different recipes are listed on the menu, but there are many more available if you know what to ask for. It is no wonder this restaurant serves 2,000 pigeons a day and over 1,000,000 a year; this is where they are raised. Here is the chance to try everything from satay pigeon to roasted Shek Ki pigeon, baked pigeon, pigeon egg with mushroom, steamed pigeon heart, and many others. In winter, try their marvellous snake soup or ask to sample the hotpot with glutinous rice and sausages. Try to avoid the crowded summer weekends and time your visit for the more relaxed weekday. To get there, drive past Shatin itself on the Taipo road and stop opposite Shatin Wo Che police station; using the overpass, you will reach the restaurant through a little aviary.

Man Wah *** 5 Connaught Road Central, Mandarin Hotel, Hong Kong, tel. 5-220111

文華廳文華酒店 中環干諾道中5號

There are some who visit the Mandarin's Chinese restaurant for its decor — a gorgeous new interior and flatteringly spacious settings that make you feel you are at an exceptionally well-behaved dinner party. Either way, the classical Cantonese cuisine is unequalled. Seasonal specialities change, of course, but look for the crispy Loong Kwong chicken with sweet walnut and deep-fried scallops or mashed wintermelon, crabmeat soup or minced pigeon in lettuce. Expensive.

**New Golden Red
Chiu Chow
Restaurant** **
13 Prat Avenue,
Tsimshatsui,
Kowloon,
tel. 3-666822

新金紅潮州酒家
尖沙咀寶勒巷13號

Chiu Chow food is not usually the favourite of
visitors. Aside from the strong Iron Buddha
tea (to match the muddiest Turkish coffee),
Chiu Chow food can be a bit too thick and
extreme as it places a lot of emphasis on offal
and blood gravy. However, those intent on
sampling this Swatow cuisine could do a lot
worse than visit the Golden Red (the 'New' is
too recent an addition for regulars to have
latched on to). Recommended dishes include
the soyed goose with fried goose blood and
vinegar and garlic on the side, a sliced chicken
with chinjew sauce, and lemon duck soup.
Another Chiu Chow dish is fried chicken balls
— good fleshy chunks of chicken formed
together with deep-fried pearl leaves. Count
this as an adventure into a particularly
individual Chinese cuisine.

Peking Garden **
Alexandra House,
Central, Hong Kong,
tel. 5-266456

北京樓
中環歷山大廈

Peking Garden is another in the Maxim's
constellation of well-groomed and efficient
restaurants offering easily readable menus
that seldom disappoint: Peking duck, beggar's
chicken, grilled hilsa herring and sizzling beef
with spring onions, shrimps with peppers, and
shark's fin soup. A word of warning on the
Peking duck is that, unless you actually
specify you want the whole bird, you will be
served the delicious skin and the rest will
disappear into someone else's equally tasty
soup. For those who have not yet watched the
noodlemaker's art, Peking Garden has nightly
displays of this not-to-be-missed culinary
cabaret. Other Peking Garden locations
include: City Plaza II, Unit 201, Taikoo
Shing, Hong Kong, tel. 5-8853555; Star
House, 3rd Floor, Tsimshatsui, Kowloon, tel.
3-698211; Empire Centre, 1st Floor,
Tsimshatsui, Kowloon, tel. 3-687879.

Sichuan Gardens ****
Gloucester Tower,
The Landmark, 3rd
Floor, Central,
Hong Kong,
tel. 5-214433

錦江春
中環置地廣場
告士打大廈3號

**Spring Deer
Restaurant** ***
42 Mody Road, 1st
Floor, Kowloon,
tel. 3-664012,
3-7233673,
3-665839

鹿鳴春飯店
尖沙咀麼地道
42號2樓

Certainly the most expensive Sichuan-style restaurant in the city, where your party of four of five could end up paying HK$250 each for an admittedly very tasty meal. Indeed, Sichuan Gardens is held in high regard by local Sichuanese themselves as serving dishes unequalled anywhere else in Hong Kong. The sizzling prawns and delicately smoked pigeon are particularly fine, but the management singles out the spiced beef and tripe with pungent sauce, camphor-smoked duck and tea leaves, and shredded beef in garlic sauce.

This is a long-time favourite with connoisseurs of Peking duck, so make sure you book ahead. The duck comes nicely browned, has a rich aroma and is served with a minimum of meat on each slab. You could try the chicken steamed with chilli and sweet peppers and then fried, or the handmade noodles. Another excellent dish is the roast shad on the hot pan or the prawns cooked with sour-hot red chilli sauce — not as dangerously spicy as it sounds.

Sun Tung Lok ***
376—382 Lockhart
Road, Ground Floor,
Hong Kong,
tel. 5-738261
(five lines)

新同樂魚翅酒家
九龍廣東道25-27號

Often mentioned in guidebooks and eulogized by food writers, Sun Tung Lok is synonymous with exotic food and, in particular, with shark's fin. The prices are high and the staff sometimes disinclined to make allowances for indecisiveness, so go in a group with at least one Chinese-speaking person and treat yourself to a feast. The abalone is delicious (and expensive) and the shark's fin supreme is self-explanatory; equally tasty is the sauteed sliced duck with walnuts. And ask for the braised cuttlefish which is scored, crisp and melting in a chilli-based sauce. Other Sun Tung Lok locations include: 137 Connaught Road West, Hong Kong, tel. 5-491137; 25—27 Canton Road, Harbour City, Kowloon, tel. 3-7220288 (five lines).

**Tai Woo
Restaurant** **
27 Percival Street,
Causeway Bay,
Hong Kong,
tel. 5-8939882

太湖海鮮城
銅鑼灣波斯富街27號
尖沙咀山林道
14-16號

These are strategically located restaurants frequented by locals and visitors alike, and they serve first-rate Cantonese food. Try the braised brisket of beef simmered for hours, vegetarian hotpot, crisp rolls of bean curd and tasty chicken, and do not forget *dim sum*, served between 11 am and 5 pm (for which no reservations are taken). The Wellington Street branch is particularly good for fish as its modified name proclaims. Other Tai Woo restaurant locations include: 17—19 Wellington Street, Central, Hong Kong, tel. 5-245688; Blocks 4 & 5, Ground Floor, North Point, Hong Kong, tel. 5-716263; 20—22A Granville Road, Tsimshatsui, Kowloon, tel. 3-7398813; 14—16 Hillwood Road, Tsimshatsui, Kowloon, tel. 3-699773.

Tien Heung Lau ****
18C Austin Avenue,
Tsimshatsui,
Kowloon,
tel. 3-662414

天香樓
尖沙咀柯士甸路18C

One of the most expensive Chinese restaurants in Hong Kong, Tien Heung Lau is spoken of in awe for its beggar's chicken and Hangchow cooking. Watch out for the short luncheon hours (noon—2.30 pm) and definitely go with a Chinese friend to help order seasonal specialities; also keep a wary eye on the price column. The management laughed when I asked to have any Chinese pop stars pointed out to me (the place is a favourite haunt) but nodded in hearty agreement when I ordered the fried white shrimp covered with Hangchow tea and deep-fried eel in its fine garlic sauce. A fine finale was a duck and *wonton* (shrimp and pork dumplings) soup — literally half a duck is cooked and boiled in a clay cauldron amidst hundreds of *wonton*. Another tip is to ask for the Chinese wine list. But again, the most useful advice is to check the prices each step of the way.

Yung Kee Restaurant **
32 Wellington Street,
Central, Hong Kong,
tel. 5-221624

鏞記酒家
中環威靈頓街32號

This is another venerable restaurant frequented by locals and serves excellent Cantonese dishes such as roast goose or scallops, and the famed hundred-year-old egg. In winter ask for snake soup with thinly sliced preserved duck, chicken and abalone; in spring, try downing the live fish, lightly steamed, or braised pigeon with bean sauce. In summer there is winter melon soup or braised abalone; autumn and winter call for rice birds. Particular recommendations from the culinary cognoscenti are the grilled prawns or scallops, and pomfret with chilli and black bean sauce.

Other Restaurants

Au Trou Normand **
6 Carnarvon Road,
Tsimshatsui,
Kowloon,
tel. 3-668754

Opened in 1964 and still thriving under the stalwart Bernard Vigneau, this homely basement bistro with its gingham table-cloths and erratic service is one of the quirkier candidates for Hong Kong's restaurant roll-call of honour. It remains a firm favourite for the simple reason that it serves good French food and, despite the almost Gallic insouciance of the waiters, is still one of the nicest places in which to meet friends and relax. There is a spaciousness that lends a Swiss rather than French feel to the informality, and the tables are a mercifully sensible size after the twee ones you usually have to shuffle the condiments around on. From the no-nonsense menu, the *hors, d'oeuvre* to favour is the home-made goose-liver mousse flavoured with armagnac; after that, fillet of sole, white wine and courgettes sauce. Or enjoy how they pass some of the truer tests such as lamb cutlets or green pepper steak. Desserts range from home-made sherberts and raspberry mousse with fresh cream to apple pancake flambed with calvados (Crepes Normandes). The cheese tray boasts 20 varieties, and a bonus comes in the *espresso* which is as good as you will have tasted and demands the companionship of a glass of calvados from which the restaurant derives its name.

Baron's Table ***
50 Nathan Road,
1st Floor, Holiday
Inn Golden Mile
Hotel, Kowloon,
tel. 3-693111 ext. 291

One of the most highly respected of hotel restaurants, the Baron's Table has, after 12 years, been completely renovated and its spry new look is a credit to all concerned. This is the place to come for rustic European surroundings and hearty German, Austrian and Swiss specialities. Also included is a 'Gourmet Health Menu' for those able to resist the regular fare or one of the seasonal promotions.

The Belvedere ****
70 Mody Road,
Harbour View
Holiday Inn, East
Tsimshatsui,
Kowloon,
tel. 3-7215161

A favourite place of many is this gourmet restaurant of the Harbour View Holiday Inn. The chef is new and the menu features fresh seafood such as crab meat cocktail with a brandy cream sauce or pan-fried sirloin steak with a spicy black pepper sauce. Also recommended is essence of pigeon with dried black mushrooms in *wonton* wrappers; and do not miss their whole range of flambes and prime cuts of beef. A huge plus is their excellent weekday business lunch and Sunday buffet that takes place to the strains of a hearteningly proficient jazz combo.

Beverly Hills Deli *
2 Lan Kwai Fong,
Central, Hong Kong,
tel. 5-265800,
    5-265809

Hong Kong's first New York-style delicatessen, the Beverly Hills Deli serves Kosher food; they even do take-outs and telephoned deliveries. The Lan Kwai Fong branch gets it right all down the line with specials galore: Texas chilli, salads, waist-watcher platters (daily Scarsdale on request), burgers, 15 spaghettis, 11 pizzas, Dr Brown's soda, root beer — the lot. Do not ask how they keep the prices down; just enjoy. Another Beverly Hills Deli is located at: 55 New World Centre, L2, Tsimshatsui, Kowloon, tel. 3-698695/6.

Bocarinos Grill ****
Victoria Hotel,
Shun Tak Centre,
Connaught Road
Central, Hong Kong,
tel. 5-407228

The Shun Tak Centre has brought considerable life to this westerly section of Central and the Victoria Hotel's European restaurant has acquired a fine reputation for international cuisine and courteous service. The decor leans towards genteel hacienda and has a feeling of space and privacy. Black caviar served with a shot of vodka makes a good starter followed by delicacies such as smoked duck breast, lobster tartelette or grilled lamb and juniper berries; particularly recommended is their soja pigeon flavoured with mango, kiwi, papaya and wild rice. The pride of the restaurant is its grills — beef, lamb, veal and venison as well as seafood —

which are cooked on an actual mesquite wood broiler. Cheese aficionados will be delighted to note that the Bocarinos board offers no less than 30 varieties. There is also a splendid Business Lunch at the bargain price of $95.

Cafe Adriatico * * *
89 Kimberley Road,
Tsimshatsui,
Kowloon,
tel. 3-688554,
3-680073

This is a genuinely charming restaurant in a pleasantly quaint setting; the staff are friendly and expert. This is part of an international chain that stems from Manila's most celebrated bistro and is rightly popular for its Spanish/Filipino cuisine. Appetizers include spiced Spanish gambas and salpicao (tenderloin cubes stir-fried with garlic and chopped celery), and the main dishes roam across a selection of seafood including calamares Biscayna and mushroom-baked sole, and grills such as a steak section devoted to 'Great Peasant Fare' and, worthy of the visit, adobo. For dessert, make for the baklava and, instead of the heady brewed Barako coffee, why not try chocolate eh, which is neither an emphatic negative nor a typographical error but stands for espeso or thick (as opposed to ah for aguado and the lighter version).

Chesa * * *
Salisbury Road,
Peninsula Hotel,
Tsimshatsui,
Kowloon,
tel. 3-666251

Hong Kong's only Swiss restaurant is a delightfully cosy haven of warm atmosphere and punctilious service. All the favourite Swiss specials are here from air-dried beef to Swiss barley soup, schnitzel, veal sausages and fondues. There are only 16 tables and you can watch closely the expression of fellow diners as they agonize over some of the miracles wrought in chocolate and listed in cruel detail on the dessert list. Expensive, and the staff say it is essential to book up to one or two days in advance.

Chili Club **
68 Lockhart Road,
1st Floor, Wanchai
Hong Kong,
tel. 5-272872

Opposite the Ramada Inn, this bustling restaurant is hot stuff in every sense of the word and was well in the vanguard when Thai food swept into vogue with Visit Thailand Year (1987). Every second breeze seems waft-heavy with the aroma of peanuts, curry paste and coconut. The Chili Club is very popular but newcomers to these dishes be warned: keep a pitcher of Singha beer nearby because they are laced with chillis, as the name suggests. Specials include spicy and sour prawn soup, satays, pineapple rice baked in the shell (a must) and the chicken/beef/pork curries with green or red curry paste, eggplant and coconut milk or Thai herbs. Essential to book in advance.

Gaddi's ****
Salisbury Road,
Peninsula Hotel,
Tsimshatsui,
Kowloon,
tel. 3-666251

A stalwart favourite of most tourists and residents who can afford it. Gaddi's specializes in gourmet cooking and the atmosphere can be a bit intimidating for the first-time customers. However, make no mistake about it, the food here is prepared with a gourmet touch and the beauty of the place could rival any Parisian restaurant. Not a single dish is bad here, and it is worth scrutinizing the 'Gaddi's Favourites' before giving way to temptation in the form of beluga caviar and lobster or the *salade d'homard*, roast rack of lamb or *entrecote a deux*. Some find the atmosphere of hauteur and genial disdain a little too brittle for honest enjoyment of a meal, but others aspire to no other life. The fact remains that no visitor who can afford the prices should miss Gaddi's; it is as much a Hong Kong institution as the 'Pen' itself.

Hugo's ***
67 Nathan Road,
Hyatt Regency
Hotel, Tsimshatsui,
Kowloon,
tel. 3-3111234

Hugo's is named after the Bavarian Baron Hugo Ludwig Wilhelm von Gluckenstein, whose fame as a host stemmed from his extravagance in serving only the best in food and wine. The very format and decor of this restaurant inspires confidence and the menu is varied to suit all tastes with dishes that combine Western cuisine with an Eastern flavour. For soup, try the artichoke bisque with three caviars; for appetizer, sliced raw Kobe beef fillet served with a choice of hot spicy tomato pepper sauce or cold mustard dressing. Seafood being one of their fortes, test the tiger prawns braised in a subtle pepper sauce with brown rice, or poached turbot with shark's fin enhanced by madeira champagne sauce. The restaurant is also well known for its U.S. prime rib of beef, wide range of seafood prepared on the open charcoal grill and the best in seasonal foods as they become available on the market.

Jimmy's Kitchen ***
1—3 Wyndham
Street, Central,
Hong Kong,
tel. 5-265293

Under the same family ownership as Landau's, Jimmy's Kitchen has been serving first-rate European food for over 50 years. Specials are shown on blackboards dotted around the room and range from rack of lamb, roast duck, pork and various souffles to pates and chicken Madras. On a slightly offbeat note, even the pickled onions on the table are famous. There is another Jimmy's Kitchen located at: 29 Ashley Road, 1st Floor, Kowloon Centre, Tsimshatsui, Kowloon, tel. 3-684027.

Korea Restaurant ***
56 Electric Road,
Causeway Bay,
Hong Kong,
tel. 5-711731

It is still not easy to find a good Korean restaurant in Hong Kong but this one is recommended. It has good beef and prawn barbecues, serves a variety of *kimchi* (fermented vegetable pickle seasoned with garlic, chilli, pepper, ginger, fish and other seafoods), peppers stuffed with beef, has excellent roasted mackerel and boasts *bulgogi* (sliced grilled beef) that is unrivalled outside Seoul. Take care over the Jinno Soju Korean wine but even if you nudge the limit, remember these are the beautiful people who brought you ginseng tea so there is no excuse for not leaving feeling well fed and invigorated. Another Korea Restaurant is located at: Ming Fai Shopping Centre, City Garden, North Point, Hong Kong, tel. 5-660706.

La Rose Noire * **
8–13 Wo On Lane, Central, Hong Kong, tel. 5-265965

So much has been made of its dark *cul-de-sac* location and jumbled signposting that La Rose Noire is now probably a more familiar site than some of its more brightly lit cousins in nearby Lan Kwai Fong. Here is an old fashioned bistro complete with a drinkers' bar and intimate tables, each sporting a black silk rose. The food is unobtrusively Gallic: starters include deep-fried camembert and snails in puff pastry, and main dishes range from pan-fried goose liver with sour cream gravy to steak tartare and grilled king prawns with garlic butter sauce. The wine list is impressively varied, as is the repertoire of Michel le patron when he settles himself at the piano and takes you musically and contented into the midnight hour.

**Landau's Restaurant ** **
257 Gloucester Road, Causeway Bay, Hong Kong, tel. 5-8912901, 5-8935876

'Nostalgic atmosphere, gastronomic delights and superb service' is how the place itself summarizes its appeal, and who can disagree? Oaken decor, genially deferential service and specials that range from medallion pork 'Lucullus' and breaded pork cutlet 'Romano' to Macau sole, baked avocado with snails and calf's liver sautéed with rosemary. Like Jimmy's Kitchen, confident, warm and always dependable — everyone's favourite.

**Maharajah
Restaurant** *
222 Wanchai Road,
Hong Kong,
tel. 5-749838,
5-8912302

As with Chinese restaurants, Hong Kong has so many good Indian ones that it is difficult to spotlight any in particular; however, the Maharajah under its beaming general manager 'Mr B', stands out. To keep the record straight, many Europeans opt for the Ashoka (57 Wyndham Street, Central) and, across the harbour, one has a choice of the plush and pleasant curries of The Gaylord (Hart Avenue, Tsimshatsui) or the veritable hive of South Indian eateries in Chungking Mansions.

What makes the Maharajah different is its variety of dishes and specialities: delicious appetizers such as mutton samosas, special Indian breads baked in their own clay oven, nine different *tandoor* dishes including the tenderest chicken tikka imaginable, seafood and vegetarian varieties and, the perfect dessert, Indian ice-cream with saffron and nuts. Attentive and friendly service and, to cap it all, at bargain prices. Its magnificent lunch buffet is a paltry HK$60 including drinks. Another Maharajah Restaurant is located at: 1−3A Granville Circuit, Tsimshatsui, Kowloon, tel. 3-666671, 3-7233344.

**The Mandarin
Grill** ****
5 Connaught Road
Central, Mandarin
Oriental Hotel,
Hong Kong,
tel. 5-220111

The management of the Mandarin tends to push their Pierrot restaurant on the top floor, but many still prefer the warm elegance of the Grill, with its burnished copper, the roast beef trolley, the pan-fried escalopes of truffled sweetbread, the fresh *agnellotti pasta* with spinach and ricotta cheese, lobsters from the tank prepared any of six ways, the broiled English farm sausages with bacon and lamb kidneys, and, of course, the sizzling steaks. Very expensive, wholly worthwhile, and essential to book if you are thinking of a weekday luncheon.

Margaux ****
64 Mody Road,
Shangri-La Hotel,
East Tsimshatsui,
Kowloon,
tel. 3-7212111
(Open noon—3 pm;
7—11.30 pm)

This elegant French restaurant was designed by Don Ashton and has a million-dollar view across the harbour. It is one of the seven restaurants in the deluxe Shangri-La Hotel and is clearly the pride and joy — which is reflected in the prices, not to mention the 28 vintages of Chateau Margaux on the wine list. The menu hints at nouvelle cuisine (sauces are light and delicate) and the preparations are finely crafted. Specialities include dill-marinated salmon, crab meat ravioli in a light shell and basil sauce, grilled guinea fowl breast with a truffle cream sauce. If in doubt, ask the head waiter. Naturally, Margaux has the usual entrees of beef (American), veal (Dutch) and garoupa (Hong Kong), not to mention bouillabaisse and a tasty lentil soup.

Ninety-seven ***
9 Lan Kwai Fong,
Central, Hong Kong,
tel. 5-260303

Mercifully less flashy than in years past, Ninety-seven still attracts the toffs but they are outnumbered by those actually interested in eating. The management is brisk and the food is of a generally high standard and cleverly served in both main course and entree portions. Tartare of salmon comes with house-baked bread, pastas are served *al dente*, there is a dream of a pork fillet, and they serve a very tasty fish wrapped in filo pastry. The dessert list has a choice of pastries, parfaits and souffles, but the home-grown sherbets are the chic choice (unless you are being deliberately unstylish in which case it had better be the galliano sabayon with zingy hazelnut ice). Slightly more middle of the road is the Brasserie underneath.

**Perfume River
Vietnamese
Restaurant** *
51 Hennessy Road,
Wanchai,
Hong Kong,
tel. 5-278644

One of the finest Vietnamese restaurants in Hong Kong and not, in fact, among the most expensive. The obvious starter is a plate of crisp prawn crackers with spiced pieces of pork followed by giant prawns, delicious spring rolls, and sausages or barbecued shrimp on sugar cane. The frog's legs in butter and sweet and sour crab are a delicacy, and there is also a very good beef curry. Pick of the day during our visit was a bowl of thick noodles. There is another Perfume River Vietnamese Restaurant at: 89 Percival Street, Causeway Bay, Hong Kong, tel. 5-762472, 5-765093.

Pierrot ****
5 Connaught Road Central, Mandarin Oriental Hotel, Hong Kong, tel. 5-220111

Everything about the Pierrot smacks of quiet elegance, and Chef Ralf Kutzner's mastery is such that it is invidious even to compare. Who are we to single out the lobster medallions with Perigord truffles and tomato mousseline from the crab soup flavoured with tarragon and mango? Or pretend that the gratinated fillet of Welsh lamb with herbs in a red bellpepper sauce takes the rosette over the roast magret of Barbarie duck in a mustard seed sauce? The smoked seabass is served with steamed celery and a light Beluga caviar sauce, the roast pigeon arrives on a parsley sauce with trumpet mushrooms, and the supreme of Bresse chicken is baked in a salt dough with fresh rosemary. All is done to perfection. Extremely expensive.

Restaurant Lalique ****
69 Mody Road, Royal Garden Hotel, East Tsimshatsui, Kowloon, tel. 3-7215215

Named after the French jeweller and artist, Rene Lalique, this decorous restaurant is set in a charming hotel. The lighting is pleasantly muted and the 30s art deco feel is pleasant and unusual. The food is haute cuisine, and specialities include the *pate de pigeonneaux aux noix*, the *filet de boeuf aux cepes sauce perigueux* and the *cote de boeuf roti a la moelle*. There is a fabulous dessert trolley, or you can choose from two flambes.

Rigoletto ***
14−16 Fenwick Street, East Town Building, Wanchai, Hong Kong, tel. 5-277144, 5-278878

This is the place to eat Italian food in Hong Kong with its comprehensive menu of northern Italian food and a vantage point from which to watch the Wanchai world go by. Some people like the piped opera music and everyone enjoys Signor Ugo, the ebullient owner-maitre d'hotel. Here is pasta a-plenty and real Italian dishes galore: the saltimbocca and grilled scampi are particularly recommended, as are the excellent stuffed lobster or escargots on garlic, many spaghettis, nigh perfect grilled liver and onions. Rigoletto has good service and a striking decor, and it is indisputably Italian. (N.B.: Those who prefer their Italian food American-style need look no further than the six Spaghetti House Restaurants. Hong Kong side: 85 Hennessy Road; 5B Sharp Street East; 10 Stanley Street. Kowloon side: 3B Cameron Road; Barton Court, Harbour City, Tsimshatsui. New Territories: Level 1, New Town Plaza, Shatin.)

Ristorante Il Mercato *
126 Stanley Main Street, Lower Ground Floor, Stanley, Hong Kong, tel. 5-8139090, 5-8139146
(Pizzeria: 5-8139239, 5-8139248)

A welcome addition to the south side of the island and a particular bonus for hungry bargain-hunters, Il Mercato and its accompanying pizzeria fill a long-felt gap. The restaurant itself is open seven days a week and serves traditional Italian dishes as well as such specialities as *risotto alla cream di scampi*, *lombato di vitello con burro e salvia* (veal) and, for devotees of pasta, *penne con peperoni freschi*. No less enticing are the various desserts and the Italian wines and liqueurs list which complete this authentic menu.

This is, in fact, the brainchild of Barry Kalb, whose enterprise and nostalgia for a proper Neapolitan pizza so hugely benefited Central's Lan Kwai Fong in the form of Marco Polo Pizza (tel. 5-216679/70). The Mercato annexe maintains the high standard: the dough is fresh- made and hand-stretched; the finest available ingredients placed on top; the whole thing baked directly on the tiles of an oven; and the menu includes Italian sandwiches and ice cream along with a seven-day-a-week delivery service to the south side of the island.

Spices **
109 Repulse Bay
Road, Repulse Bay,
Hong Kong,
tel. 5-81222711

Some lament the old Repulse Bay Hotel, but *carpe diem*, I say, and let us be grateful that somewhere as nice as Spices came out of the renovation. Decorated with taste and featuring a pan-Asian menu of the best of spicy dishes, this is a clever idea that works well. Order a cooling *lhassi meethi* (yoghurt blended with milk and rose water) as you await your spicy prawn soup with lemon grass (a copywriter's dream, the menu has this Thai dish under 'Cauldrons of the East'), followed by *tabouleh* (cracked wheat, tomato and parsley salad) or perhaps a *fritada baboy* from the Philippines. Everything pleases here, from the friendly staff to the colonial ambiance evoked by high ceilings — not to mention the convenience of a spacious on-premise car park.

Stanley's Restaurant ***
86–88 Stanley Main
Street, Stanley,
Hong Kong,
tel. 5-8138873

Stanley has the honour of having been one of the very few settlements on Hong Kong before the British arrived in 1842, but it took some years to get a Western restaurant. The wait was worth it: Stanley's serves excellent food, looks like the private home it once was, and is owned by three Europeans of whom at least one is usually around to greet guests. There are seven separate dining areas on three floors, including two balconies and a private room — and the fresh air and sound of the surf complete the idyll. There are *a la carte* menus, an inexpensive set lunch menu and a *menu de degustation* for dinner. Specialities shown on the blackboard change daily. Stanley's is open from morning to night 364 days a year and is deservedly popular enough to require booking for weekends and public holidays. What could be more pleasant than to follow a successful foray in the market with a delicious meal or tea and then an easy ride back to Central, watching the view from the swaying upper deck of a No. 6 bus? For those who drive, there is a parking service.

The Steak House **
18 Salisbury Road,
Regent Hotel,
Tsimshatsui,
Kowloon,
tel. 3-7211211

The Regent chain has always been in the forefront of interesting restaurants, and the Hong Kong Regent is no exception. The Steak House is an all-American treat: American charcoal grilled steaks (nine choices), all-American salad bar (about 20 ingredients of the freshest kind), even American desserts like grasshopper pie, plus one of the finest selections of American wines to be found in Asia. Very tasty and filling, and the salad buffet is an innovative treat for weight-watchers. It is just a shame that one must order the steak to qualify for the salad. The view across the harbour is as distracting as ever and the service punctilious.

The Regent Hotel also has a continental restaurant, La Plume, which counts among its various specially created dishes cream of artichoke with Beluga, salad of rock lobster and bay shrimp in an homardine sauce, and sauteed paupiettes of sea perch in a champagne butter sauce. If you have to ask the price you cannot afford it!

Tomowa Japanese Restaurant ***
6 Percival Street,
Ground and 1st
Floors, Causeway
Bay, Hong Kong,
tel. 5-8336339

This excellent Japanese restaurant has separate entrances at street level, so decide if you want to sit at a counter on the ground floor, or enjoy a meal in a cosy booth in one of the four rooms on the first floor. The staff are friendly and attentive, the atmosphere relaxed and very much the real thing. As for the menu, the cuttlefish with crab eggs could not be faulted and the *sushi* and *teppanyaki* set dinner were exactly as desired. Other gems included the seasonal *namaebi* (live prawn) and the *Tomowa yosenabe* (lobster, abalone, trough shell and a selection of seafood and seasonal vegetables cooked at the table).

Hotels

Hong Kong has some of the best hotels in Asia, perhaps the world, in terms of comfortable, well-equipped guest rooms, efficient and friendly service, imaginative decor, marvellous views and top notch facilities for wining, dining, meeting and relaxing.

At the end of 1987, Hong Kong had more than 21,000 hotel rooms, of which 16,970 were classified as 'high tariff' by the Hong Kong Tourist Association. More hotels are under construction, and almost every week brings news of yet another opening, ground-breaking or site bought for hotel development. Amazingly, occupancy throughout 1987 averaged 90 per cent and for much of the year it remains impossible to book even a single room at short notice.

Whichever hotel you choose in the top categories, it will be a modern high-rise building with air-conditioned rooms which include private bathroom, telephone, colour television and often a refrigerator and mini-bar. The odds are that the views will be spectacular. Keen competition keeps the standard of service very high and most hotels have round-the-clock room service.

Hotels in the moderately priced category are clean, comfortable and efficiently staffed. They tend to be a little farther from the tourist hubs but are well served by taxis and public transport.

All hotels have good restaurants. The smaller ones might have one dining room, serving European and Chinese food. The large hotels contain some of the best restaurants in town (see Restaurants, page 171), where much local expense-account entertaining takes place.

The hotels also are used extensively for business meetings, conferences, art exhibitions, trade promotions and special events such as antique auctions.

The following list offers a brief description of some of Hong Kong's hotels. All add 10 percent service charge and five percent tax to the bill. Listing is in alphabetical order. Rates are in Hong Kong dollars.

Hotels: A Selected List

Hotel	Description	Facilities
Central		
China Merchants Hotel 160 Connaught Rd W. tel. 5-596888	A conveniently located high-rise with three restaurants, and two bars, this is good value for money with double rooms ranging from HK$460–$620.	3 restaurants, 2 bars, conference room, health centre

Furama **Inter-continental** 1 Connaught Rd C. tel. 5-255111	An elegant high-rise with 571 rooms beside the harbour, close to ferry and MTR. It has busy meeting areas and a spectacular revolving restaurant. Rates HK$1,000—$1,350 for a double.	4 restaurants, 3 bars, revolving restaurant, disco
Hilton 2A Queen's Rd C. tel. 5-233111	Centrally located with 800 rooms, popular restaurants and a superb pool terrace. It has regular dinner-theatre presentations. Rates HK$1,110—$1,420 for a double.	4 restaurants, 6 bars, pool, Brigantine cruises, business centre
Mandarin 5 Connaught Rd C. tel. 5-220111	In easy reach of Central offices, a hub for local and visiting businessmen. Famed for service, restaurants and Roman-bath. It has 565 rooms at HK$1,300—$1,750 for a double.	5 restaurants, 3 bars, health club and pool, business centre
Victoria 200 Connaught Rd C. tel. 5-407228	This hotel boasts spectacular harbour views for 75 percent of its 540 rooms and 330 apartments. HK$850—$1,050 for a double.	3 restaurants, lobby lounge, music room, pool, health club and business centre

Causeway Bay

Caravelle 84—86 Morrison Hill Rd, Happy Valley tel. 5-754455	Opposite the racecourse, a convenient, comfortable and moderately priced hotel, 102 rooms at HK$460—$575 a double.	Bar, restaurant, coffee shop
Excelsior 281 Gloucester Rd tel. 5-767365	Next to the cross-harbour tunnel and close to shops, restaurants and nightlife. Famous for its nightclub and sports facilities. Its 926 rooms are HK$800—$1,250 a double.	3 restaurants, 3 bars, nightclub, tennis courts, health club
Harbour 116—118 Gloucester Rd, Wanchai tel. 5-748211	On the waterfront, close to nightclubs and restaurants, a friendly and reasonably priced hotel with 200 rooms at HK$400—$600 a double.	Nightclub, bar, 2 restaurants
Hong Kong Cathay 17 Tung Lo Wan Rd tel. 5-778211	In Causeway Bay, a quiet, comfortable hotel with 142 rooms, moderately priced at HK$402—$448 a double.	Restaurant, coffee shop
Lee Gardens Hysan Avenue tel. 5-8953311	Close to the nightlife and shops of Causeway Bay, the hotel has large public areas and 809 rooms at HK$800—$950 a double.	3 restaurants, 3 bars
New Harbour 41—49 Hennessy Rd tel. 5-8611166	Newly renovated with 173 rooms in the heart of Wanchai with good food and atmosphere. Rates are HK$450—$630 a double.	Restaurant, coffee shop, lobby bar
Park Lane 310 Gloucester Rd tel. 5-8903355	Opposite Victoria Park and close to busy Causeway Bay, its 850 rooms range from HK$950—$1,400 a double.	2 restaurants, disco, gallery lounge, coffee shop, sauna, massage

Kowloon

Ambassador Nathan Rd/Middle Rd tel. 3-666321	At the head of Nathan Road, close to shops and nightclubs, a friendly hotel with 315 rooms, HK$690−$910 a double.	2 restaurants, coffee shop, bar, nightclub
Empress 17−19 Chatham Rd tel. 3-660211	Convenient to downtown Kowloon and the airport with 189 rooms. Rates are HK$550−$800 a double.	Coffee shop
Fortuna 351−361 Nathan Rd tel. 3-851011	In the busy Mongkok area, catering to Southeast Asian groups with 193 rooms, good food and rates of HK$560−$760 a double.	2 restaurants, business centre
Grand 14 Carnarvon Rd tel. 3-669331	In the centre of the entertainment area, a good reliable hotel with 194 rooms at HK$660−$820 a double.	2 restaurants, bar
Holiday Inn Golden Mile 50 Nathan Rd tel. 3-693111	On the shoppers' 'Golden Mile', a superbly run hotel with good bars and restaurants and 599 rooms at HK$990−$1,120 a double.	3 restaurants, bars, business centre, pool, sauna
Holiday Inn Harbour View 70 Mody Rd tel. 3-7215161	New in East Kowloon, with good views of the harbour, the hotel has first class food and 600 rooms at HK$860−$1,190 a double.	5 restaurants, bar, pool, health club, business centre
The Hongkong Hotel 3 Canton Rd tel. 3-676011	A favourite with business visitors, next to the Ocean Terminal and Star Ferry, the hotel has superior food and 790 rooms at HK$780−$990 a double.	3 restaurants, 4 bars, pool, health club
Hyatt Regency 67 Nathan Rd tel. 3-3111234	Lively and efficient, a hotel close to the Kowloon action, known for Hugo's restaurant, it has 723 rooms at HK$770−$1,400 a double.	4 restaurants, 3 bars, night club, business centre
International 33 Cameron Rd tel. 3-663381	Convenient and comfortable, a hotel long known for moderate prices, it has 154 rooms at HK$460−$750 a double.	Restaurant, bar
Kowloon 19−21 Nathan Rd tel. 3-698698	Opened in January 1986, and part of the Peninsula Group of hotels, it has 707 rooms at HK$570−$610 a double.	2 restaurants, bar, coffee shop, business centre
Marco Polo Harbour City, 13 Canton Rd tel. 3-7215111	A member of the Peninsula Group, with 441 rooms at HK$630−$900 a double.	3 restaurants, bar, pool, health centre, sports centre
Miramar 130 Nathan Rd tel. 3-681111	A city within a city, a hotel with three wings and numerous facilities, it has 542 rooms at HK$800−$980 a double.	11 restaurants, 5 bars, theatre, supperclub, business centre, convention centre
Nathan 378 Nathan Rd tel. 3-885141	An unpretentious hotel at the top of the 'Golden Mile', the Nathan is convenient and inexpensive with 186 rooms at HK$370−$540 a double.	4 restaurants, snack shop, bar

New World
New World Centre
22 Salisbury Rd
tel. 3-694111

On the edge of Kowloon Bay next to a vast
new shopping and entertainment complex,
the hotel has 735 rooms at HK$820 a double
and good public facilities.

2 restaurants, coffee
shop, bar, pool

Park
61–65 Chatham Rd
tel. 3-661371

An old favourite for its large rooms and
comfortable bar-lounge, the hotel is well
located. It has 450 rooms at HK$600–$800 a
double.

2 restaurants, coffee
shop, bar

Peninsula
Salisbury Rd
tel. 3-666251

The grande dame of Hong Kong hotels with
its famous lobby and fabled restaurants, the
Pen has 210 rooms at HK$1,450–$2,100 a
double.

5 restaurants, bars,
lobby lounge,
business centre

Prince
Harbour City
tel. 3-7237788

Next to a major shopping centre, the Prince
has 402 rooms at HK$750–$850 a double.

2 restaurants, bar,
lobby lounge and
business centre

Regal Meridien
East Tsimshatsui
tel. 3-7221818

A member of the Air France-Meridien chain,
this 590-room hotel has rooms at
HK$1,090–$1,290 a double.

5 restaurants, 2 bars,
lobby lounge, disco

Regal Meridien
Kai Tak Airport
tel. 3-7180333

Hong Kong's first airport hotel has 384 rooms
at HK$750–$1,050 a double.

4 restaurants, coffee
shop, 2 bars

Regent
Salisbury Rd
tel. 3-7211211

A hotel with royal box views of the harbour,
a breathtaking lobby lounge, superb
restaurants and 602 rooms at
HK$1,250–$1,950 a double.

5 restaurants, bars,
lobby lounge, pool,
health club, business
centre

Riverside Plaza
Tai Chung Kiu Rd,
Shatin
tel. 0-6497878

This 830-room hotel, opened in May 1986,
has a shuttlebus service to Shatin Station and
New Town Plaza as well as Tsimshatsui.
Rates HK$700–$900 a double.

3 restaurants, coffee
shop, bars,
health-care centre,
disco and swimming
pool.

Royal Garden
East Tsimshatsui
tel. 3-7215215

A member of the Mandarin International
group, it features a huge garden atrium lobby.
With 433 rooms, rates are HK$800–$1,250 a
double.

4 restaurants, coffee
shop, rooms overlook
indoor garden

Shamrock
223 Nathan Rd
tel. 3-662271

For budget travellers, this hotel is
comfortable and convenient, with 150 rooms
at HK$370–$450 a double.

Restaurant and bar

Shangri-La
East Tsimshatsui
tel. 3-7212111

A deluxe hotel managed by Westin, it has a
fabulous decor, a fine French restaurant and
719 rooms at HK$1,125–$1,850 a double.

4 restaurants, coffee
shop, bars, lobby
lounge, pool sauna,
business centre.

Sheraton
20 Nathan Rd
tel. 3-691111

Overlooking the harbour and at the head of
the 'Golden Mile', this hotel is noted for its
business facilities and international cabarets.
It has 922 rooms at HK$1,030–$1,580 a
double.

5 restaurants, disco,
nightclub, 8 bars,
pool, business centre

Recommended Reading

A wealth of literature and information has been published about Hong Kong. For authoritative historical background, Maurice Collis' *Foreign Mud* (Faber & Faber, 1964) and G.B. Endacott's *A History of Hong Kong* (Oxford University Press, 1973) are excellent.

Hong Kong's strange genesis and stranger survival is described in *Borrowed Place, Borrowed Time* by Richard Hughes (Andre Deutsch, 1968). Hughes was a veteran reporter who lived in Hong Kong for almost 30 years and his book offers an intriguing and highly readable account of the place.

Austin Coates is one of Hong Kong's leading historians with a lucid and attractive style. Among his books are *Myself a Mandarin* (Frederick Muller, 1968; Heinemann (Asia) 1975) which describes his years as a magistrate, and *Whampoa* (South China Morning Post 1980) the history of local shipping.

For history, anecdote and some magnificent photographs, try *Hong Kong: The Cultured Pearl* by Nigel Cameron (Oxford University Press, 1978) and for some fascinating insights into the traditional life of rural China, Hugh Baker's two-volume *Ancestral Images* (South China Morning Post, 1979) is a winner.

The Hong Kong Government has published many excellent books dealing with different aspects of the territory. Of special note are *This is Hong Kong: Temples* (1977) with detailed descriptions of 12 Chinese temples, and *Rural Architecture of Hong Kong*, which illustrates in words and pictures some of the historic buildings still surviving in the New Territories.

For an indispensable reference book, the government publishes an *Annual Review*, packed with statistics, analysis and superb picture essays on just about every aspect of Hong Kong — all official, up-beat and reliable.

James Clavell has fictionalized the leading characters and machinations of the great hongs, or trading companies, in *Taipan* (Dell, 1966) and *Noble House* (Hodder & Stoughton, 1981). Both required exhaustive research but the facts have not been allowed to spoil a good adventure story.

The same applies to two other books with a Hong Kong setting. John Le Carre's *The Honourable Schoolboy* (Hodder and Stoughton, 1977) is a spy thriller featuring some recognisable local residents. Robert Elegant's *Dynasty* (Collins, 1977) is an exciting and highly fanciful saga of a Eurasian family very loosely based on a local clan. .

Index